SATURDAY'S CHILD

Ellen Fairclough is perhaps best known as the first woman in Canada to become a federal cabinet minister. John Diefenbaker appointed her Secretary of State in 1957. In the course of her career she also served as Minister of Citizenship and Immigration and Minister responsible for Indian Affairs, and was in charge of the National Gallery, the National Film Board, the Dominion Archives, and the National Library. She was also a chartered accountant, a business woman, a local politician in Hamilton, and a wife and mother. At a time when many people believed that a woman's place was in the home, she successfully balanced family obligations with a career in the largely male world of federal politics.

Writing with the style and wit for which she was famous as a politician, Ellen Fairclough, now ninety, tells her story. Her reminiscences describe her early life, her efforts to become a business woman, and her experiences as a Progressive Conservative member for the constituency of Hamilton West (1950–63). Fairclough discusses the political factors that led to her appointment to the Diefenbaker cabinet, as well as other factors, including family values and the opportunities available in the bustling industrial city of Hamilton, that served as the context for her successes. While her story focuses on the politics involved, Fairclough also writes extensively about family life, friendships, and domestic detail. She attributes her success to the fact that she was a 'Saturday's child' who worked hard for what she achieved.

The source of much media attention during her political career, Ellen Fairclough was often the only woman in a room full of men and, on one occasion, was asked to leave a cabinet meeting because the topic of discussion - sexual assault - might be too rough for her sensitive ears. Having no female role models to follow, Fairclough made her own rules and charted her own course. These memoirs make a fascinating contribution to the history of women and poitics in this country.

ELLEN LOUKS FAIRCLOUGH, Member of Parliament for Hamilton West (1950–63), was made a Companion of the Order of Canada in 1995.

MARGARET CONRAD, professor of history at Acadia University, has written extensively on the history of women and twentieth-century political developments in Atlantic Canada, and is the author of *George Nowlan: Maritime Conservative in National Politics*.

ELLEN LOUKS FAIRCLOUGH

Saturday's Child: Memoirs of Canada's First Female Cabinet Minister

With an Introduction by Margaret Conrad

UNIVERSITY OF TORONTO PRESS

Toronto Buffalo London

© University of Toronto Press Incorporated 1995
Toronto Buffalo London

Reprinted 1995, 2017

ISBN 978-0-8020-0736-0 (cloth)

ISBN 978-1-4875-9842-6 (paper)

Printed on acid-free paper

Canadian Cataloguing in Publication Data

Fairclough, Ellen
   Saturday's child : memoirs of Canada's first
   female cabinet minister

   Includes index.
   ISBN 978-0-8020-0736-0 (bound). – ISBN 978-1-4875-9842-6 (pbk.)

   1. Fairclough, Ellen. 2. Cabinet ministers –
   Canada – Biography.* 3. Women government
   executives – Canada – Biography. I. Title.
   FC616.F3A3 1995   971.064'2'092   C95-931660-4
   F1034.3.F3A3 1995

Cover photo: Bill and Jean Newton Photography,
City of Ottawa Archives

University of Toronto Press acknowledges the financial assistance to its
publishing program of the Canada Council and the Ontario Arts Council.

This book has been published with the help of a grant from the Ellen Fairclough
Foundation.

Every effort has been made to obtain permission to reproduce the photographs
that appear in this book. Any errors or omissions brought to our attention will
be corrected in future printings. Unless otherwise indicated, photographs are
from the Fairclough family collection.

Contents

Introduction

While watching news coverage of the Progressive Conservative Party's leadership convention held in June 1993, I was surprised to see eighty-eight-year-old Ellen Fairclough, the first woman to sit in a Canadian federal cabinet. She moved the nomination of Kim Campbell, who emerged as party leader and first female Prime Minister of Canada. Since all eyes were on Campbell, viewers learned little about Ellen Fairclough. Nor, it turned out, had anyone bothered to document her pioneering contribution to Canadian political life. Was this yet another example of the Canadian tendency to ignore its heroes? The next day, I wrote to Mrs Fairclough to inquire if anyone had been commissioned to tell her story. If not, I brazenly asked, would she be prepared to grant me an interview to discuss my writing her biography? She replied immediately. Not only was she prepared, without having met me, to let me be her biographer; she had a 75,000-word memoir that would speed my progress. Apparently, two well-known Toronto publishers had turned down her manuscript, one editor telling her quite bluntly, 'we could not find anyone who ever heard of you.'

I made arrangements to meet Ellen Fairclough at her Stanley Avenue home in Hamilton later that summer. When I arrived, a few minutes early, Ellen was in the basement ironing her sheets. As a baby-boomer, prepared to suffer the hardship of sleeping with wrinkles, I was suitably impressed by this display of domestic standards and disciplined work habits. I was also struck, like many people before me, by Ellen's erect carriage, quick movements, and infectious smile. In short order, I was introduced to her husband, Gordon – her friend and fan for nearly seventy-five years – and whisked off to the Hamilton Club for a leisurely lunch. The Faircloughs were generous hosts and congenial companions. Since they had a previously arranged engagement later that day, I left with the rejected manuscript tucked securely under my arm.

I spent the rest of that sunny, summer afternoon at a nearby Hess Street restaurant, sipping Perrier water and reading 'Saturday's Child.' It was a good read. While the manuscript needed some editorial attention, it was crisply written and gave a clear picture of the major developments in Ellen Fairclough's long life. Surely, I reasoned, this document, written in the ninth decade of her life by one of Canada's significant 'first' women, deserved a better fate than to be mined for information by academic vultures such as I. Having read the memoirs of several of her political colleagues, I recognized Ellen Fairclough's manuscript as both more economical in length (thank goodness!) and less structured by research advisers than is often the case. This was no long-winded effort to chronicle great achievements or to rewrite history, but an honest attempt to describe the progress of a life by a woman who sees it as 'bad manners' to take oneself too seriously.

Having an academic interest in women's autobiographical writing, I immediately recognized other features of Ellen Fairclough's memoir that made it special. Scholars are now beginning to distinguish a woman's way of seeing the world that reflects the affective and emotional relationships that typically have defined women's role in society.[1] Thus Ellen Fairclough, chartered accountant, civic leader, and federal politician, devotes more space in her memoirs to family life, friendships, and domestic detail than one would expect to find in the reflections of a man with a similar career profile. Many people reading Ellen's manuscript, perhaps even the editors who had earlier turned it down, would argue that it is 'thin' because it places too little emphasis on political analysis and too much on private matters.

In writing her memoirs, Ellen was concerned with telling her life story,[2] not with providing an analysis of her contribution to politics. As such, this

1 The debate on this issue was brought into focus by Carol Gilligan in her innovative study *In a Different Voice: Psychological Theory and Women's Development* (Cambridge, Mass., 1982).

2 On this topic, see the pioneering work of Estelle C. Jelinek, *The Tradition of Women's Autobiography: From Antiquity to the Present* (Boston, 1986), and her earlier, edited volume, *Women's Autobiography: Essays in Criticism* (Bloomington, Ind., 1980).

book is a significant contribution to our understanding of how a woman who came of age in the 1920s became a successful wife and mother, business woman, and member of Parliament at a time when few women of any class or culture in Canada could 'do it all.' Ellen Fairclough quite correctly attributes her success to the fact that she was a 'Saturday's child,' who worked hard for what she achieved, but other factors also played a role. In particular, the family and community context in which she worked were critical to the way her life unfolded. She describes this context in some detail in the following pages.

The history of women in formal politics in Canada is confined almost entirely to the twentieth century. Ellen Fairclough was thirteen years old when laws were passed in 1918 to permit women to vote in federal elections. Prior to her successful bid for the constituency of Hamilton West in April 1950, only five women had managed to win seats in the House of Commons.[3] None had been appointed to the cabinet. How did Ellen Fairclough succeed where others had failed?

The answer to this question lies, in part, in the history of the Conservative Party in Canada. Despite efforts to make itself attractive to the electorate, the party of Sir John A. Macdonald had difficulty winning elections in the first half of the twentieth century. The Liberals characterized their opponents as the party of big business, Ontario, and the British connection, a description that contained more than a grain of truth. In the general election of 1940, the Liberals under William Lyon Mackenzie King swept to victory with 184 seats, while the National Conservatives managed to win only 40 seats, 25 of them in the Tory heartland of Ontario. Even their leader, Robert Manion, lost his seat. Refusing to be consigned to oblivion, committed Tories made yet another attempt to reinvent their party to appeal to Canadians.[4] At their leadership convention in Winnipeg in 1942, they chose John Bracken, the Progressive Premier of Manitoba, as their leader, approved a 'progressive' platform, and adopted the name 'Progressive

---

3 A recent study by Sydney Sharpe, *The Gilded Ghetto: Women and Political Power in Canada* (Toronto, 1994), usefully surveys the fate of women in the formal political arena.

4 Larry A. Glassford, *Reaction and Reform: The Politics of the Conservative Party under R.B. Bennett, 1927–1938* (Toronto, 1992); J.L. Granatstein, *The Politics of Survival: The Conservative Party of Canada, 1939–1945* (Toronto, 1967).

Conservative' for their party. The party won only 68 seats in 1945, again mostly in Ontario, but the trend was, for them, in the right direction.

Under George Drew, the Ontario Premier who was chosen national leader in 1948, Progressive Conservative organizers positioned their party to topple the Liberals. In their efforts to do so, they made a special pitch to women voters. Ellen Fairclough was targeted as a possible winner in Hamilton West. She did not disappoint and, indeed, probably surprised the 'backroom boys' with her vote-catching ability. Although she lost in Hamilton West in the general election of 1949, she was able to win a by-election the following year. Once in the House, she proved her worth and could not be ignored when John Diefenbaker led the party to victory in 1957. Despite his suspicions that she was one of his 'enemies,' he appointed her to the Secretary of State portfolio.

Ellen Fairclough's elevation to the cabinet came a generation after women in Great Britain and the United States made a similar breakthrough. In 1929 Margaret Bondfield, a seasoned political activist, was appointed Minister of Labour by the governing Labour Party in Great Britain. Four years later, in the United States, Democratic President Franklin Roosevelt chose social reformer Frances Perkins to be his Secretary of Labor.[5] Ellen Fairclough also served as Labour critic for the Progressive Conservatives when they occupied the Opposition benches, but, for reasons revealed in the following pages, she was not Diefenbaker's choice for that portfolio.

While Ellen was the lone woman in a cabinet of men, she was not the only woman in Canadian politics. Women became involved in formal party structures as soon as they were granted suffrage, but they were relegated to auxiliaries and supporting roles rather than to the front lines of party activity.[6] Ellen served her time in the lower ranks, working actively in the Ontario Young Conservatives in the 1930s. In the following decade she became involved in Hamilton civic politics, often the first rung of the political ladder for women. She also raised money for the party and, as an accountant, worked closely with a number of key figures in Hamilton's business and professional circles.

5 Bondfield titled her memoirs *A Life's Work* (London, 1948). Although Perkins produced no autobiographical account of her career, she published *The Roosevelt I Knew* (New York, 1946) as well as a policy analysis, *People at Work* (New York, 1934).
6 Sylvia B. Bashevkin, *Toeing the Lines: Women and Party Politics in English Canada*, 2nd ed. (Toronto, 1993), chap. 3.

Although other Canadian women worked in the back rooms of political parties and served on town councils, they did not become cabinet ministers. A number of factors combined to enable Ellen Fairclough to break through the 'glass ceiling' that had hitherto blocked women's advancement in federal politics. Among the most important influences on her life was the family in which she was raised. Agnes Macphail, Canada's first woman MP, once quipped, 'Perhaps if I owed my father the ability to get into Parliament, I owed my mother the ability to stand it when I got there.'[7] In slightly different words, Ellen Fairclough makes the same point about her own family, in which her father, Norman Cook, was clearly the head of the family but her mother, Nellie Louks, was the solid centre, keeping boarders to make money, urging regular attendance at Zion Methodist Church, and counselling her five surviving children with truths passed down from her Huguenot ancestors. Ellen learned lessons in family responsibility early in life, most notably during the devastating influenza epidemic that hit Hamilton in late 1918, and applied what she learned to both her private and her public activities.

The city of Hamilton was the crucible in which Ellen Fairclough's political career was forged. The Cooks – migrants to Hamilton from rural Norfolk County in 1904 – were among the thousands of people attracted to urban centres during the industrial boom that swept Canada at the turn of the century. With its steel mills and branches of American firms, Hamilton in 1904 offered many opportunities to those willing to work hard and take risks.[8] Norman Cook was prepared to do both. He worked as a contractor in the housing boom that accompanied the doubling of Hamilton's popula-

7 Margaret Stewart and Doris French, *Ask No Quarter: A Biography of Agnes Macphail* (Toronto, 1959), 27.
8 There are several excellent scholarly sources on the history of Hamilton in the post-Confederation period, including John C. Weaver, *Hamilton: An Illustrated History* (Toronto, 1984), and Brian Palmer, *A Culture in Conflict: Skilled Workers and Industrial Capitalism in Hamilton, 1860–1914* (Montreal, 1979). Craig Heron, *Working in Steel: The Early Years in Canada, 1883–1935* (Toronto, 1988), provides much valuable information on the steel industry in Hamilton. Michael Katz, *The People of Hamilton, Canada West: Family and Class in a Mid-Nineteenth Century City* (Cambridge, Mass., 1975), offers glimpses of Hamilton society in an earlier period. See also *Dictionary of Hamilton Biography*: vol. 1, to 1875 (Hamilton, 1981); vol. 2, 1876–1924 (1991); vol. 3, 1925–1939 (1992); and vol. 4, 1940–1965 (forthcoming).

tion from 51,527 in 1896 to 104,330 in 1916. Given the seasonal and cyclical nature of the construction industry, it is not surprising that Ellen remembers the family fortunes rising and falling in her childhood years.

The uncertainty of economic existence in an industrial city served as an incentive for all members of the Fairclough family to contribute in some way to the household income. Although Ellen excelled at school and was an accomplished pianist, she harboured no illusions about an academic or artistic career. She began part-time work at the age of twelve and entered the full-time labour force when she was only sixteen years old. With her succession of clerical jobs, concern for fashion, and participation in community activities, she was a typical 'girl of the new day,' who embraced the possibilities open to women in the 1920s.[9] Ultimately, Ellen's life course deviated considerably from that of her mother and grandmothers. She postponed marriage to stay in the labour force, moved beyond the narrow possibilities of secretarial work to the mysteries of stock brokering, and joined a wide range of voluntary organizations. By the time she married Gordon Fairclough, in 1931, she had invented herself as a business woman, pillar of the Anglican church, and partner in an equal-relationship marriage. She was a woman who made things happen rather than a victim of custom and circumstance. Despite the 'talk' of her middle-class neighbours, she returned to the workforce soon after her son, Howard, was born and took correspondence courses to earn her accreditation as an accountant. She 'hung out her shingle' in 1935, in the depths of the Depression. With her husband's encouragement and support, she became active in the Conservative Party. Her business activities expanded during the Second World War, and she began to travel widely. Clearly no ordinary 'married lady,' she soon attracted the attention of Conservative organizers in her city and province.

Today more women follow the life course chosen by Ellen Fairclough, but at the time of her election to the House of Commons in 1950 she was an exceptional woman. The media covered her achievements in the same breathless tones that were used to chronicle the activities of sports and movie stars. In Ottawa she was often the only woman in a room full of

9 Veronica Strong-Boag, *The New Day Recalled: Lives of Girls and Women in English Canada, 1919–1939* (Toronto, 1988) and 'The Girl of the New Day: Canadian Working Women in the 1920s,' *Labour / Le Travail*, 4 (1979), 131–64.

men, and, on at least one occasion, she was asked to leave a cabinet meeting because the topic – sexual assault – was deemed too rough for her tender, feminine ears. Having no role models, she made her own rules and charted her own course. This memoir tells us how events looked to her from this unique vantage point.

Maintaining that the facts speak for themselves, Ellen Fairclough is exceedingly modest about her achievements. It is important to remember that Ellen Fairclough was a pioneer in virtually everything she did. In addition to her acknowledged accomplishments in politics, she was one of Canada's first female certified accountants,[10] assumed executive positions in several prominent voluntary organizations, and established successful businesses both before and after her career in federal politics. Her determination to take advantage of opportunities that began to emerge for women in twentieth-century Canada sets her apart from the majority of women in her generation. An exceptionally bright and talented child, she excelled in school and, had she been a boy, would almost certainly have been singled out for a career in medicine, law, or, in light of her mathematical skills, accountancy. As a girl, she was forced to choose a more circular route to worldly success, but in the end she triumphed over the obstacles placed in her path because of her gender.

In editing Ellen Fairclough's memoirs, I have attempted to alter them as little as possible. My intrusions consisted of rearranging portions of the material to fit more neatly into the chronological sequence of the chapters, adding information on people and events for the convenience of the general reader, and in a few cases acknowledging sources. I have also helped Ellen to select photographs from her magnificent collection to supplement the written word. In an effort to provide the reader with the flavour of earlier times, I have included several newspaper accounts of Ellen's public activities. These have been carefully preserved in her scrapbooks, which are now housed in the Special Collections Division of the Hamilton Public Library.

10 Reginald C. Stuart, *The First Seventy-Five Years: A History of the Certified General Accountants' Association of Canada* (Vancouver, 1988); Philip Creighton, *A Sum of Yesterdays: Being a History of the First One Hundred Years of the Institute of Chartered Accountants* (Toronto, 1984).

I have also added information on the fall of the Diefenbaker government, much of it drawn from the typescript of an interview conducted with Mrs Fairclough in 1968 by York University history professors J.L. Granatstein and Peter Oliver. Although I was occasionally tempted to ghost-write certain sections of her story, I have resisted doing so. It would then become my story, not her own.

Ellen was nearly eighty-five years old when she finished her memoirs. Had she written them following her defeat at the polls in 1963, she might well have highlighted different aspects of her life and described political events with a more critical edge. By 1990, time had blurred many of the petty details of political life while at the same time bringing other incidents into bold relief. Ellen's manuscript ends with a series of stories about people and events that now matter to her. To these I have added a number of anecdotes that she included in earlier chapters but that seemed to interrupt the narrative. Together they offer insights on the life of a woman who now looks back in awe and amusement on a long and active life.

Over the course of many delightful hours spent with Ellen and Gordon Fairclough, I have probed them on a number of topics that remained unexplored in these memoirs. I have no doubt that they find my questions embarrassing, perplexing and, on occasion, downright rude. How did family members respond to your achievements? Why did you become an Anglican upon marrying Gordon? Why did you not have more children? How much money did you make? How did women voters in Hamilton respond to your candidacy? What is your view of the women's movement? Who bankrolled your election campaigns? What was your relationship with organized labour in Hamilton? Tell me more about the 'dirty tricks' that Hamilton elections are famous for, and so on.

These are questions that come from an academic trained in the questionable art of digging beneath the surface of daily events to uncover the 'real' story. In a few instances, I have added information provided by Ellen in response to my probing, but, as she openly admits – 'least said, soonest mended' – her silences are often as revealing as her comments. Readers of these memoirs must wait for the biography of Ellen Fairclough for answers to questions that interest me. For those who want to compare the published version of this memoir with the manuscript that I first read in a Hess Street restaurant, the manuscript is deposited in the Ellen Fairclough Collection, housed in the Hamilton Public Library. Most people will be surprised by how little I have changed the original.

At the request of the University of Toronto Press, I have added brief introductions to the four sections of the memoir to set the context for the stages in Ellen Fairclough's life. There are, of course, many contexts that could be discussed, and no historian writing in the postmodern era would dare to claim that such intrusions into the narrative are anything but a tribute to one's own ego. Nevertheless, I have chosen four themes that help to frame Ellen's experiences – Hamilton in the early twentieth century, women's work in the interwar years, federal politics during the Cold War, and the women's movement of the 1960s. Readers interested in Ellen's story might prefer to develop their own contexts of interpretation.

Despite my minimal involvement in this effort, I have a long list of people to whom I am indebted. The officers of the Division of Research and Graduate Studies, Acadia University, were sympathetic to my request for the seed money necessary to follow up my initial letter of inquiry to Mrs Fairclough. Financial support for preparing the manuscript for publication was provided by the Association for Canadian Studies (ACS) through funds made available by the Canadian Studies Directorate of the Department of Canadian Heritage. Without this assistance, 'Saturday's Child' and many other Canadian manuscripts would still be collecting dust. The ACS is to be congratulated for supporting Canadian culture in this important way.

I am also grateful to Jack Granatstein for permission to use portions of the interview that he and Peter Oliver conducted with Ellen Fairclough in 1968 as part of their work for the York University Oral History Programme. Much of the material in the Prologue and chapter 9 is based on these interviews. I also consulted the transcript of an interview with Ellen Fairclough conducted by Peter Stursberg in 1973 as part of his research for his two-volume work on the Diefenbaker era to compare Ellen's versions of events.[11]

A number of people close to Ellen and Gordon have been most generous with their time and patient with my persistent questioning. I want to thank in particular George Davidson, Margaret Green, Mary and Joan Heels,

---

11 Peter Stursberg, *Diefenbaker: Leadership Gained, 1956–62* (Toronto, 1975) and *Diefenbaker: Leadership Lost, 1962–67* (Toronto, 1976). Transcripts of Mr Stursberg's interviews are housed in the National Archives of Canada.

Joyce Mongeon, and Jim and Daisy Moodie and to warn them all that they have not seen the last of me. J. Brian Henley, Head of Special Collections at the Hamilton Public Library, and his staff have been courteous and helpful. They have not seen the last of me either.

I am deeply grateful to University of Toronto Press editors Gerry Hallowell, Rob Ferguson, and John Parry, who supported this project, despite my sullen resistance to much of their good editorial advice. I am also grateful to Colleen Golding, Pat MacNutt, and Brenda Naugler, who helped to get the manuscript ready for the press by producing an index, wrestling with the laser printer, and kicking the photocopier. My student assistants, Brian Clarke and Trevor Head, also performed valuable editorial services. Gary Boates of Acadia University's Audio Visual Services division did much of the photographic work required for the publication. I am indebted to James W. Brennan, Archivist, Visual and Sound Division of the National Archives of Canada, and David Bullock, Assistant Archivist, City of Ottawa Archives, for helping me to locate copyright information on photographs used to illustrate the memoirs, and all the copyright holders who were so generous in granting permission to publish their work. Finally, I wish to thank my colleagues Doug Baldwin and Barry Moody, my mother, Gladys Slauenwhite, and two of Ellen's close friends, Margaret Green and Daisy Moodie, each of whom read the manuscript in its entirety for style and grammar. Any remaining errors are, of course, due entirely to the fact that I continued to tinker with the prose after they had made it perfect.

Margaret Conrad
Acadia University
April 1995

Preface

One of the jingles that we quoted as children ran thus:

Monday's child is fair of face,
Tuesday's child is full of grace,
Wednesday's child is full of woe,
Thursday's child has far to go,
Friday's child is loving and giving,
Saturday's child works hard for a living,
But the child that is born on the Sabbath-day
Is brave and bonny and good and gay.

I have seen other versions, but this is the one that was accepted when I was young. On top of one of my bookshelves stands a small piece of ceramic art that depicts a little girl knitting, and, through an aperture in its base, there appears the inscription 'Saturday's child works hard for a living,' so I have some evidence that my version is correct.

In any event, I am a Saturday's child, having been born on 28 January 1905, the fourth child (third living, there being one infant death) of Norman Ellsworth Cook and Nellie Bell Louks. I have had a long and wonderful life, with a balance of successes and failures, comedies and trage-dies, obstacles and rewards. Although I never got rich, I have had exhilarat-ing adventures, happy friendships, and, from my dear husband, Gordon, life-sustaining love. I worked hard for a living, but I grew through my labours and had the privilege to become, in 1957, the first woman to serve in a federal cabinet in Canada. From this position, I came to a new understanding of how hard a Saturday's child could work!

Most women in Canada work hard for a living, and it is only in this century that they have begun to break through the laws and customs that made it difficult for women to exercise their rights fully as citizens. Women were denied the right to vote in federal elections until 1918, and it was not until 1929 that the Persons Case acknowledged that women were indeed 'persons' in the eyes of the law. This momentous decision came as a result of an extended crusade by the 'Famous Five' women from western Canada – Emily Murphy, Henrietta Muir Edwards, Nellie McClung, Louise McKinney, and Irene Parlby – who fought their battle all the way to the Privy Council in Britain, which, prior to 1949, was the final court of appeal in the Canadian judicial system. Until 1929 Canadian women were citizens under the law in matters of 'pain and penalty' but not in 'rights and privileges.' They were therefore denied appointments to the Senate and even had their judicial positions called into question. So unfriendly was the democratic process to women's involvement that only one woman, Agnes Macphail, elected for the Ontario constituency of Grey County in 1921, managed to get elected to the House of Commons in the 1920s.

The Famous Five were rewarded for their persistence on 18 October 1929, with the judgment of Lord Sankey, the Lord Chancellor, who ruled: 'The British North America Act planted in Canada a living tree capable of growth and expansion ... their Lordships have come to the conclusion that the word "persons" in Section 24 includes members both of the male and the female sex, and that, therefore, the question propounded by the Governor General must be answered in the affirmative, and that women are eligible to be summoned to and become members of the Senate of Canada.' It was a remarkable victory for these indomitable crusaders and, of course, for all Canadian women. In the following year, Prime Minister William Lyon Mackenzie King appointed Cairine Wilson to the Canadian Senate.

On the fiftieth anniversary of this historic decision, the federal government honoured women by establishing the Persons Award. Five Canadian women are chosen annually to receive a commemorative medallion, sculpted by Dora de Pedery-Hunt, and a citation of their achievements. It was after one of these ceremonies that Maureen McTeer had a luncheon in the Parliamentary Restaurant in my honour. The group consisted of Ruth Bell, Grete Hale, and Daisy Moodie. George Hees 'crashed' the party for a short while, and discussion soon revolved around the many amusing experiences that we shared when we were colleagues in the House of Commons. The pressure was then on 'to write a book.'

'You should write a book!' is a comment frequently made to people in public life. I cannot begin to count the number of times that it was said to me. For a long time I paid no attention, largely because I was much too busy with other activities. I also doubted in my own mind that people would really be interested in anything I had done. After the luncheon discussion, I began seriously to consider writing my memoirs, but I hardly knew where to start. I dithered. Maureen and Grete persisted, particularly Grete, who would not let me off the hook, and it is largely due to her encouragement that I have tried to record some of the highlights of my life.

Writing one's memoirs is not an easy task. Since the mind is a faulty computer, dates, names, and the sequence of events are often elusive. Research and writing take time and require strict discipline. Some of the events are painful to recall. On many occasions I was tempted to do anything other than put my fingers to the keyboard of my trusty Smith-Corona portable. I received a number of suggestions, such as, 'Rent a cottage up north,' 'Hide away in Greece' (they tell me that's what writers do), 'Disconnect your telephone and lock yourself in your room.' Since I am a crank about my domestic duties, such writing strategies were out of the question.

A serious delay resulted from the grave illness and subsequent death of our dear son, Howard, in 1986, just eight days after his fifty-fifth birthday. He had suffered from lung cancer for some time and had undergone excruciating treatment, but, on the occasion of his birthday, he seemed much better. For most of the previous week he had performed in the musical portion of the Scottish Rite program, and we heard reports to the effect that 'the music was out of this world.' For the first time in many months we had hope. In retrospect, I am sure that he had some premonition that the end was near and made a superhuman effort to 'put on a good show.' Mercifully, the end was very sudden.

The stress of Howard's illness almost certainly contributed to Gordon's slight stroke and subsequent heart condition, which has, of necessity, slowed us down and curtailed many of our activities. However, I have persevered in this task, and it is my hope that in these pages readers will find something to stir memories, provide some amusement, and contribute to the understanding of Canada's rich history.

Ellen Louks Fairclough
Hamilton, Ontario
April 1995

Acknowledgments

Anyone who has ever written a book knows what a frustrating and time-consuming job it is. With a very full calendar of events, and ongoing household duties, I could find little quiet time for writing my memoirs. In order to get the job done, I had to forgo many meetings and social engagements in which I had great interest. I hope that those who have been the recipients of regrets will understand and forgive me. Because of my project, Gordon, too, has had to make excuses. He has also been most helpful in fielding telephone calls and saving me from ill-advised comments, but, of course, he could not catch them all and cannot be blamed for anything found herein.

A number of close friends have also sustained me through my lonely career as a memoir writer. Lorne MacKay, who passed away early in 1994, read the manuscript and offered comments. Jim and Daisy Moodie remembered details of my parliamentary career, and Margaret Green helped me to recall events of my years at Hamilton Trust. All of the above-mentioned people, together with my good friend Joyce Mongeon, kept up the pressure to 'get on with it,' and I am grateful to them for their persistence. Ivan King, the best neighbour in the world, has always been there when we needed him, as have Michael and Faye Ng of the Forbidden City restaurant who have offered us food and friendship over the years and have been especially kind to us when we were busy or unwell.

When it looked as if the final product would never reach the standard required by a publisher, Margaret Conrad wrote to me – literally out of the blue – and offered to edit the manuscript. I am grateful for her efforts on my behalf. Finally, J. Brian Henley, Head of Special Collections at the Hamilton Public Library, organized my papers and scrapbooks, which served to jog my memory. The professional touch provided by Mr. Henley and his staff made my job of recording past events much easier, and I am indebted to them for their help.

SATURDAY'S CHILD

Prologue:
The Fateful Day

The day I was offered a cabinet post remains firmly etched in my memory. Immediately after John Diefenbaker was asked by Governor General Vincent Massey to form a government, all of the aspirants to office began to converge on Ottawa. I should not say 'all,' because a few obviously had more pride and good sense. Those who did make their way to the capital haunted the antechamber to the Prime Minister's office. There they sat, I am told, for hours on end (no pun intended). Of course, reporters watched these comings and goings, making guesses as to who would get what post. I have since learned that some of this waiting was at Diefenbaker's instigation. He would ask a prospective minister to come at 9:00 a.m. and then leave him there all day. At 6:00 p.m. he would say, 'Come tomorrow at 9:00.'

I remained at home, with no intention of going to Ottawa. I felt then as I do now: 'It's good manners to wait until you are asked!' I must admit that I could not see how Diefenbaker could do other than ask me, because he had made a point of saying during the campaign that he would put a woman in the cabinet. Margaret Aitken from the Toronto riding of York-Humber was the only other woman elected in 1957, and we joked about which of us he would call. Since I had the longer service in Opposition and had chaired various committees, we both agreed that mine was the stronger claim. (He could, of course, have appointed both of us, but such a possibility was out of the question in those days!) There were, as well, women he could have called from outside the caucus, but he would have had to open a seat for them, and this would have brought forth a storm of protest from my constituents and created unnecessary bother for his minority ministry. So he was pretty well stuck with me.

I make this statement advisedly, because John Diefenbaker did not like me. Our differences of opinion on matters of party policy were deeply rooted. He never forgave me for the anti-Communist stand that I took at an annual meeting of the party in 1940. While he himself was opposed to Communism, he nevertheless took an academic view of it and felt that any opposition would only drive Communists underground. I, in contrast, felt that our party had nothing to lose by taking a strong public stand, because the big bosses of the Communist Party, with the exception of Tim Buck, were underground already. We had a long, hard-hitting, and bitter debate; then, as always, he took it very personally when anyone opposed him. He never forgave me for the stand I took and frequently made pointed remarks about 'those who fought against me at the annual meeting in 1940.' I knew what he meant, and he knew that I knew what he meant.

He also had not forgiven me for refusing to support him in his bids for party leadership in 1942, 1948, and 1956. In the period leading up to the Leadership Convention in 1956, Margaret Aitken and I had talked the matter over at some length, and we felt that, as the only two Progressive Conservative women in Parliament, we could not support any candidate openly. It would be construed as a bid for the women's vote in favour of that candidate and would then be unfair to the other candidates and possibly have negative repercussions for women in the party. I still think that we were right.

Donald Fleming also solicited my open support. Although we had been friends for many years – back to the 1930s, when we were both active in the Young Conservatives of Ontario – I refused to join his camp. He understood my position, and we continued to be good friends. I did not support Davie Fulton publicly, but I voted for him. My reasoning would not impress Diefenbaker. I felt that Davie was a young man who had a great career ahead of him. If he got only a handful of votes, it would have been hard on his ego and possibly detrimental to his future prospects. I tried to persuade Davie not to run for the leadership, but he was adamant.

While I did not support Diefenbaker in his bid for party leadership in 1956, I was not among those who set out to undermine his candidacy. However, he always had a bunch of people hanging around him who had axes to grind, and subsequent events have confirmed me in my opinion that at least some of these people swung their axes dangerously close to my head.

The formation of a federal cabinet has never been an easy task for a Canadian Prime Minister. With so many regional, cultural, and personal interests to placate, a leader must have the wisdom of a Solomon to get it just right. It also has to be done quickly after an election so that the business of government can be efficiently handled. Within a few days of the election on 10 June, Dr William (Bill) Blair, the popular member for Lanark, died. It had been thought that he would be appointed to Health and Welfare, and his death threw everyone into a panic. I went to Ottawa, as did a large number of newly elected MPs, and was then going to go to Perth, where the funeral was to be held. George and Fiorenza Drew telephoned me at the Château Laurier Hotel, where I was staying, and asked if I needed a ride to the funeral. I accepted their invitation, and we had a good talk along the way.

As former leader of the Progressive Conservative Party, and a particular target of Diefenbaker's animus, George Drew was keen to know who was in and who was out of the cabinet. He asked if the Prime Minister had called me yet. When I said, 'No,' he and Fiorenza laughed, and he said, 'Well you shouldn't be driving with us then – it may not be understood.' I replied, 'I couldn't care less,' and I meant it.

At the cemetery, Diefenbaker motioned with his head for me to come over to his side. He asked me if I could see him later in the day. I said, 'Yes. When?' We finally decided upon 6:00 p.m., in his office. I was there on time, but he kept me waiting, while various people, mostly members of his staff, ran in and out of his private office. It was difficult to tell what was going on. After about half an hour, he called me in and asked me to sit down. 'Well,' he said, 'I have to form a cabinet, and it looks as if I shall have to form it largely of my enemies.' I thought, 'Least said, soonest mended,' and said nothing, which seemed to surprise him somewhat.

He then went into a rambling discourse, talking about his many problems. In the course of his remarks, he accused me of having been an active supporter of Donald Fleming at the convention. I told him bluntly that he was wrong, that I had not actively supported anyone but that I had voted for Davie Fulton, and I told him why. I also told him that anyone with half an eye could see that he would win the leadership, so it was no great credit to the bandwagon boys. (I remember a remark made at the convention by Frank Lennard, the member for Wentworth, who said, 'Look at those monkeys barking their shins, climbing on the bandwagon.')

'Loyalty, complete loyalty,' is what he expected, he said. If I came into his cabinet, I declared, he would have my loyalty, and any time I could not be loyal to him I would get out, pronto. I have never stayed in a job where I could not give my boss the fullest loyalty and cooperation. I also told him that I was not a person to hold grudges and that many of my close friends were people with whom I had been unable to see eye to eye at one time.

Diefenbaker made some remark about my warm friendship with the Drews. This was a good example of how relationships change, I said, indicating that at one time George and I had been bitter enemies. He was greatly surprised, and had to admit that despite past differences I had given George my complete support during his years as leader of the party. So I suggested to him that he might like to ask George about our past associations. I do not know whether he did, but I think that little piece of information set him back on his heels.

'Well, you can be Secretary of State,' he said eventually. This announcement surprised me, but I tried not to show it. There were other portfolios that I had thought would be more appropriate to the experience I had gained while in Opposition – Labour or possibly Health and Welfare. I simply said, 'Well, I shall let you know.' Back in my room at the Château Laurier, I called the Drews. George let loose with a juicy expletive, which covered the situation nicely. I proposed calling Diefenbaker and telling him, 'No dice.' George's response was characteristically direct and convincing. 'Don't be a *** fool. You won't be in that portfolio for long, and remember, you will be the first woman cabinet minister in Canadian history.' The next day I called Diefenbaker and thanked him for the appointment. (In the light of Diefenbaker's attitude towards me, I was surprised when he told me a year or so later, in the course of some conversation about departmental matters, that he recognized and appreciated my loyalty.)

On 21 June 1957, I was sworn into office as Secretary of State for Canada. But George Drew had been right: I was not Secretary of State for long. Immediately after the 1958 election, the Prime Minister called on a Sunday evening to ask if I would accept the portfolio of Citizenship and Immigration. I demurred to the extent of saying, 'That is a very difficult portfolio,' to which he replied, 'I know it is very difficult, but you are very competent and can handle it.'

When I went into his office after being sworn into my new post, he said, 'You must be tough – don't let them push you around.' I did not know who 'they' were, but it is true that in Citizenship and Immigration I was pushed and pulled by all and sundry, both inside and outside government. In addition to being responsible for immigration, which was becoming an increasingly contentious issue in postwar Canada, I was Superintendent General of Indian Affairs, an important area of Canadian life that really warranted its own separate portfolio. I was also responsible for five federal agencies: the Dominion Carillonneur, the National Film Board, the National Gallery, the Public Archives/National Library, and the Royal Canadian Mint. It was an experience – nearly four and a half years – such as I never expected to have. On more than one occasion, I said to myself, 'What's the use?' I came so close to resigning that the slightest additional weight might have tipped the scales. However, I had my personal staff to consider, all of whom would have been out of a job if I quit. Moreover, I knew that if I threw in the towel, the criticism would have been levelled at all women – 'She couldn't take it.' I find this to be a common comment when the woman in question has been carrying an exceptionally heavy load. Finally, I was too stubborn to quit. My reaction was, 'I'll be damned if I'll let them taunt and abuse me into resignation.' In that case I would just be giving in to them, and by 'them' I meant the whole kit and caboodle: Opposition, media, and public.

I had a fairly tough hide when I entered politics, but it grew to be two feet thick by the time I retired from public life in 1963. In my final months in office, during the minority government of 1962–63, I held the portfolio of Postmaster General, which brought with it its own special headaches. By that time the Diefenbaker ministry was so beset by external criticism and internal squabbling that life in cabinet had become intolerable. The Diefenbaker government, and I personally, suffered defeat at the polls in the April 1963 election. Thereafter, I resumed my business career in Hamilton. I was not altogether sorry to be out of the political fray and to exchange the endless days in politics for busy days in business.

PART ONE

Coming of Age in Hamilton

1905–1931

IN THE FIRST TWO CHAPTERS of her memoirs, Ellen Fairclough recalls what it was like to grow up in Hamilton in the early decades of the twentieth century. Change and opportunity were hallmarks of the bustling industrial city at the western end of Lake Ontario. A city of 54,000 souls in 1901, it grew to 77,000 by 1911 and reached over 200,000 by 1951. Many of Hamilton's residents came from Ontario and other parts of Canada, but an increasing number – nearly 40 per cent by 1931 – were immigrants, mostly from Great Britain and continental Europe. The immigrants were trans-forming the face of a city incorporated at a time when men such as Family Compact stalwart Sir Allan MacNab dominated local political and cultural life. Although Hamilton's Loyalist roots continued to be celebrated, new elites, with different historical memories, were gradually making their mark on the social and political scene.

In 1911, half of Hamilton's labour force was employed in manufacturing. Two steel companies, Stelco and Dofasco, emerged to achieve dominance, but a wide range of lighter industries, such as International Harvester, Otis-Fenson Elevator, and Westinghouse, also located in Hamilton at the turn of the century. In the wake of boom and bust cycles associated with the industrial economy, commercial, construction, and service businesses expanded and contracted. Some 15 per cent of the workforce was unemployed during the postwar recession of 1921–2, the worst of the 'bad times' before the Great Depression of the 1930s.

Identities based on class, ethnicity, and religion were reflected in Hamilton's geography. Elite citizens clustered against the 'Mountain,' while the suburbs emerging outside the city's core beckoned to the upwardly mobile. In working-class districts, people sorted themselves out in ethnically distinct communities. The segregation of Hamilton's populace was a deliberate policy, reinforced by custom and law. Historian John Weaver, in *Hamilton: An Illustrated History* (Toronto, 1984), reports that in 1913 Italian labourers working on city streets were spat upon by men riding by on the streetcars (p. 93), and when the fashionable suburb of Westdale was developed after the First World War, covenants forbade sales to Blacks, Jews, and the foreign-born (p. 103). Strikes often dissolved under the acid test of ethnic tensions in the labour force, and even the gangs that emerged to control bootlegging and gambling between the wars were based on ethnic alliances.

Family and church were the lenses through which young Ellen Cook viewed Hamilton, and her angle of vision was shaped by her own particular experiences. Thus she remembers the First World War less for the terrible loss of life on the battle front or the industrial boom and social tensions it brought to Hamilton than for the flu epidemic that forced her to assume family responsibilities at an early age. Five hundred Hamiltonians died during the onslaught, making it very much the dramatic and tragic event that Ellen recalls.

When Ellen was a youngster, the Methodist church in Canada was deeply involved in the social gospel movement. Its goal was to improve people's worldly condition as well as save their immortal souls. Given her age and family focus, Ellen remembers Zion Methodist Church for the athletic and social activities it sponsored rather than for its work among the city's burgeoning working class. Nevertheless, the reformist outlook championed by the Methodists influenced Ellen. It accounts in part for her humanitarian efforts in voluntary associations and helped to put her in the ranks of 'progressive' Conservatives when she became active in politics.

From our vantage point in the late twentieth century, Ellen received remarkably little formal education. After she completed grade eight at the age of thirteen, she entered the commercial stream taught in Hamilton schools and graduated three years later ready to earn her way in the world. In making this choice, Ellen was typical of most young women in Canada at the time who opted for the trio of occupations largely reserved for women: teaching, nursing, and secretarial work. The last-named was the easiest and shortest route to employment for women, and, given the uncertainty of her family's finances, it is not surprising that Ellen took it.

Ellen's chronicle of the many jobs she held between 1921 and 1931 reveals the wide range of secretarial opportunities available to young women in Hamilton in the 1920s. Retail establishments, municipal government offices, automobile tire companies, and banking and brokerage offices all required skilled clerical help to manage the growing volume of documents on which the new industrial order floated. Ellen was an ambitious and enthusiastic recruit to the new bureaucratic processes, increasingly making her mark by her ability to 'fix' people's muddled financial records. It was this skill that she eventually parlayed into an accounting career.

Nellie and Norman Cook with Cecil and Rhea c. 1900

Two years old

With Howard (left) and Rhea (centre) at 322 Hunter Street West, 1908

Alexander Louks, 'the only grandfather I ever knew'

'Aunt Jen's gift,' 11 November 1918

With a class of Sunday School students c. 1921

A 'girl of the new day,' 1926

En route to New England, 1929

1

School Days and Sundays

The flu epidemic descended upon Canada in the final year of the Great War, striking almost every family in Canada with varying degrees of intensity. At the time, our household consisted of my father and mother, two sisters, a brother, and two male boarders. My father and one of the boarders were spared, as was I. How I managed to escape, I do not know, but, as a consequence of my continuing good health, I had to look after my mother, two sisters, and a brother, who were all in bed with the flu at the same time. (Our boarder waited a couple of months before succumbing to the plague, by which time mother was fully recovered and able to take care of him.)

In addition to caring for four desperately ill people, I had three hungry men to feed three meals a day: an early breakfast because they had to be to work by eight o'clock, a substantial dinner when they came home at noon, and a supper at the end of the workday. In between meals I had to make beds, give medication, and offer general nursing aid, including taking temperatures at regular intervals and supplying plenty of fluids. It was quite a job for a thirteen-year-old.

Our family doctor, Dr J. Heurner Mullin, was very concerned about me. When he came to the house he carefully instructed me on spraying my nose and throat regularly and advised me to wear a mask when I was in the rooms of my patients. One day, as he was leaving, he said, 'Whatever you do, don't get it.' I didn't – I was too busy.

It was impossible to get any help, either nursing or domestic. My father, an exceedingly good housekeeper, helped with the dishes and other chores when he came home from work. He could cook, sew, and polish floors (which he loved to do), and he often tackled the mountains of laundry that piled up from the many patients. Although she had her own household to look after, my sister-in-law Stella (the wife of my brother, Cecil) came over one day to see what she could do to help. She decided to make a blueberry pie, and when she emptied the fruit out of the bowl, she licked it. She was invariably proper, and I was so surprised by her bad manners that I laughed. I think that is why she did it – I must have looked very forlorn.

As the foregoing suggests, the flu epidemic taught me lessons in family responsibility at an early age. I consider myself fortunate to have grown up in a large and close family whose roots are deeply embedded in the soil of Upper Canada. When I was young, family history counted for something in establishing one's status in southern Ontario, and those with the proper pedigree were quick to make it known. I am fifth-generation Canadian through both parents, a fact in which I take considerable pride.

On my mother's side, I am descended from Henry Crouse Louks and his wife, Sarah Sluyter. They were Huguenots and United Empire Loyalists who moved with their three-year-old son, William, to Norfolk County from Vermont in 1790. The name was originally De Laux or Du Laux but was spelled in a variety of ways, including 'Luck,' 'Luke,' and 'Laux' without the 'de,' obviously the result of phonetic spelling where the written record did not exist. William Louks married Huldah Huffman, and their son Alexander was my grandfather. Alexander married Ellen Steinhoff (for whom I am named), and their daughter, their sixth child, Nellie Bell, was my mother. She married my father, Norman Ellsworth Cook, on 25 June 1889.

On my paternal side, I am descended from Andrew and Anna Cook, who emigrated to Ancaster, Upper Canada, in 1802 from Lancaster, Pennsylvania. Andrew applied for a grant of land and was given 200 acres in Toronto Township in 1808, but he did not move his family there until 1816. His son Jacob, at the age of nineteen, had settled there a year earlier, after voluntary service in the War of 1812. This family helped to found the town of Cooksville. Although I had been vaguely aware of having many relatives, it was not until John and Eileen (Shepherd) Houser published a genealogical sketch of the descendants of Andrew and Anna Christina (Palmer) Cook in 1970 that I discovered the names of over 2,000 of them in my father's family. Captain Fred Cook, my first cousin (once removed), now a resident of Tillsonburg, with the help of many other Cooks, is continuing this research.

Andrew and Anna Cook had twelve children. Their second child, Elizabeth, married a woodsman named Compeign. This is all that we know about him except that he was killed in a logging accident a few months after their marriage, leaving Elizabeth pregnant. According to the family story, Elizabeth had married against the wishes of her brother Jacob. Though her junior by five years, Jacob was the eldest son and took over as head of the family following Andrew's death. Jacob promptly disowned Elizabeth, probably because Compeign was both French and Roman Catholic. Since religious conviction ran deep in Methodist families like the Cooks, Elizabeth was written out of the family for her choice of a husband. When it became known that she was widowed and pregnant, Jacob refused to receive her into the family home (Jacob was not then married). Prevailed upon by family and neighbours, he replied, 'I have no sister.' Of course, he had other sisters, but, at least in this dramatic account, he referred expressly to Elizabeth. Finally, it is said, a Roman Catholic priest convinced Jacob to 'do right' by his sister. But there were strings attached. 'You may come home,' Jacob is reputed to have told his sister, 'but your son, when he is born, will be my son and bear my name.' (It apparently never occurred to him that the child might be a girl!) So it was that Luke became Jacob's adopted son and, in the course of time, my own grandfather.

Luke married Mary Hamilton in 1845. They had seven children, the youngest being my father, Norman Ellsworth Cook. There is a twenty-five-year span in age between Norman and his eldest brother, Henry, so I had first cousins about the same age as my mother. Norman married Nellie Bell Louks and I am the third of their five surviving children: Cecil (born 1890), Rhea (1896), myself (1905), Howard (1906), and Mary (1908). Between Cecil and Rhea there was a son named Leo, who died in infancy.

Luke and Mary Cook settled in Norfolk County on a farm purchased for them by Jacob. Luke added to his holdings and also, I am told, had a store in Delhi (then called Fredericksburg). When the store was destroyed by fire in 1878, Luke returned to the farm. Luke was Justice of the Peace in Fredericksburg and, in that capacity, issued the marriage licence for my father and mother in 1889. In the same year, Luke helped found the Frederick Lodge, No. 217, A.F. & A.M., which he served as first Worshipful Master. As a tribute to him, the Frederick Lodge later secured a photograph of him, which it sealed hermetically in his tombstone in the Delhi graveyard.

My father also farmed in Norfolk County but was literally 'blown off' the land. Since the light soil was not conducive to good yields (before tobacco), he took a construction job with the railway. In October 1904, he moved his family to Hamilton, where he purchased a house at 322 Hunter Street West, at the western edge of the city. I was born at home at eight o'clock on Saturday morning, 28 January 1905. My father subsequently became a contractor, building many houses in the rapidly expanding west and north ends of the city. During the winter, when construction slowed down, he took wage-paying jobs, one of which was cutting ice on Burlington Bay (Hamilton Harbour). The large blocks of ice were stored between straw in ice-houses to be used in warmer weather.

In December 1912 we moved a few blocks to a new home, which my father built for the family at 12 Tuckett Street. He also built a house next door (14 Tuckett) for my mother's sister, Agnes Jordison, who was blind. She lived there until her death. My father constructed a cement walk from her back door to ours to help her feel her way with her feet. A rather 'touchy' individual, she could, when she felt herself offended, march briskly along the walk without bothering to 'feel her way,' an achievement that caused our family great amusement. Aunt Agnes was also an accomplished musician, having received musical training at the Brantford School for the Blind. As a young woman she had quite a musical career. Indeed, she was touring the United States with the Salvation Army when she met and married Thomas Jordison, a man some fifteen years her junior. Music remained an important emotional outlet for Aunt Agnes, who, when taking offence at our house, would return home to her piano, where she would vent her feelings for at least an hour. We all enjoyed the music, although that was not what she intended.

Aunt Agnes played an important role in my young life, most particularly by encouraging in me a great love of reading. She herself was an avid reader, having parcels of books in Braille sent to her every week. From the time I moved to Tuckett Street at the age of seven, she had me read aloud to her. I still treasure the leather-bound volume of Tennyson which was her Christmas present to me in 1917, and which, many times, we read and wept over. For some reason, we found the story of Enoch Arden particularly poignant. The original leather binding has since worn out and been replaced, but I can still feel the soft nap of the original, which I held for many, many hours, while she sat in her rocking chair and listened.

I had been reading since the age of five, when I received my first school book. It was a family joke that it was no use talking to me when I was reading because I simply could not hear and read at the same time. I recall taking books to bed with me and reading them under the covers with the aid of a flashlight. In my youth I read the Bible from cover to cover several times (except the 'begats') and developed a love of poetry and biography. Later in life I became a 'whodunit' fan and never travelled without a murder mystery in my briefcase.

Music was important in our family. From an early age I took piano lessons from my older sister, Rhea, and later I polished my skills with formal lessons in both piano and organ from Robert Symmers at the Hamilton Conservatory. As an adult I occasionally played the organ at Zion Methodist and later at St George's Anglican churches. In 1931, when I was carrying my son, Howard, I even performed the *Kamennoi ostrow* by Anton Rubinstein at Recital Hall in Hamilton. I also had a knack for drawing and was often singled out in school for some artistic effort or another. Before I was married I dabbled in oils and watercolours, evidence of which still hangs on the walls of our home. However, I never seriously considered following my artistic bent because it did not offer much financial security.

Alexander Louks was the only one of my grandparents I ever knew. Since my father was the youngest of his family and my mother the second youngest of seven children, the other grandparents were gone before I arrived on the scene. Grandfather Louks lived with us for several years until his death in 1917. He told us many stories, which we were not wise enough to record, a fact Rhea and I regretted in later years. One of my fondest memories is of him singing 'Beulah Land' while sitting in his rocking chair. Like many members of his family, he was quite a musician and had organized a brass band in Delhi by dint of teaching all of its members to play their instruments.

When he was in his sixties, he was very ill with what was diagnosed as a 'tumour of the lung' and was not expected to live. His home in Delhi was just a block or so from the town hall, where, he claimed, the band practised the 'Death March' in preparation for his funeral. He loved to tell the story, rocking away in his chair, amused by the fact that he had 'outlived them all.'

Because I was named for my grandmother Louks, my mother gave me my grandmother's locket, which contained pictures of both her and grandfather. These pictures must have been taken in 1860 by an itinerant photographer who arrived as grandmother was nursing her baby, my Aunt Jen, who was born 30 December 1859. My mother drew my attention to the blouse, which is partly unbuttoned and must have been buttoned in a hurry when the photographer arrived. The pictures are tintypes, with colouring, now faded, applied to the cheeks. If the pictures were taken in 1860, my grandmother and grandfather would have been twenty-two and twenty-eight years of age, respectively, and they already had Jen and a three-year-old daughter, my Aunt Aggie, who was either born blind or became so shortly after birth. The locket itself has several small dents, having been used as a teething ring by successive babies.

We come from a long-lived family. Although my father died at seventy-five, his eldest brother, Henry, lived to the age of ninety-six. My mother celebrated her eighty-ninth birthday, and her father lived to be eighty-five. This pattern ran through the families of both my parents. My father had another brother, Clarence, who died only three months short of his one-hundredth birthday. With the exception of my elder brother, Cecil, who died at the age of seventy-five, all other members of my immediate family lived beyond their eightieth birthdays.

I was the eldest of my parents' 'second family.' Cecil and Rhea were respectively fifteen and nine years older than I, while Mary, Howard, and I came quickly over a period of less than four years, between January 1905 and August 1908. Despite our differences in age I was close to Cecil and admired my 'big' brother, who eventually owned and operated a pharmacy on Dundurn Street. Mary and I were also close. We shared a room until I left home, and later she worked with me in my business and political activities. Rhea taught me piano. In fact, she taught me so well that I earned one of the highest marks (82) in primary grade piano in an exam administered by the Hamilton Conservatory. My younger brother, Howard, enjoyed a long career with Bell Telephone.

My father and mother had a warm relationship. One story that my mother used to tell offers some insight into his attitude. My father said one day, 'I wish I had someone I could play chess with,' to which my mother replied, 'Well, Norman, why don't you teach me?' And he said, 'Hell, Nell, you're too dumb.' My mother, far from being offended, found this story amusing. While it is true that my father was a clever man, my mother also had her 'smarts.' In addition to raising the five of us, she kept boarders to add to the family income, and throughout she maintained her sense of humour. My mother frequently used sayings that stemmed from her youth in Norfolk

County, which had been settled largely by Pennsylvania Dutch and Huguenots. Her favourite saying was, 'A dog that brings a bone will carry one,'
which she applied to any bit of derogatory gossip. In his book, *The Trail of
the Black Walnut* (revised edition, Toronto 1965), G. Elmore Reaman
includes six pages of such sayings, to which I could add a few.

On the whole, I enjoyed school and was a good student. I attended nearby
Ryerson School for kindergarten and my first eight grades. Although we
never went hungry, we were not an affluent family. Money was often hard to
come by, especially when 'hard times' descended on Hamilton, which they
seemed to do periodically. I can remember as a young child being embarrassed because we could not always afford to pay our school fees. From grade
one onward, children were required each month to pay ten cents, which the
teacher then marked off against our respective names. I presume she then for-
warded it to the School Board. Mother had the practice of knotting the precious dime into the corner of a handkerchief so that it would not be lost on
the way to school. If I remember correctly, it was early in 1914, when I was
nine years old, that I was told we could no longer afford the fees. Since there
were three of us of school age by that time, it meant thirty cents out of the
family coffers. We were not the only family in that position, but I will never
forget my embarrassment. It was the only time that I can remember the family economy letting us down so completely. My older brother, Cecil, was a
struggling pharmacist with family responsibilities of his own, while Rhea,
who taught music, found fewer students to teach in difficult economic times.

Fortunately for our family, conditions in Hamilton improved with the
outbreak of the First World War. Although the war did not touch our family
directly, it had a dramatic impact on Hamilton, whose steel plants and other
industries were kept pretty busy producing for the war effort. I can remember
the excitement on the day that the armistice was signed, which was also the
day that I sat for a photographer's portrait, a gift to me from my Aunt Jen.
Perhaps she felt that I deserved a present after my own battles with the flu
epidemic.

During the last three years in public school, we had the same teacher,
which was unusual, but then Miss (Jessie) Kennedy was an unusual teacher.
She was a small woman of Scottish ancestry, which showed occasionally in
her speech. Despite her size and gentle manner, she never had any disciplin-
ary problems in her class. I do not recall anyone, boys or girls, receiving more

than demerit marks. My scholastic rival was Grace Taylor, who was very stu-
dious. She excelled in history, which I hated – all those dates – while I was
much better in mathematics. We see-sawed back and forth for first place
throughout those three years. Grace went on to Collegiate and later became
a school teacher. She must have been influenced then, and subsequently, by
Miss Kennedy. Several years after her retirement, a group of her former
pupils, led by Jean Simpson (who had married Herb Grover) and me, organized a dinner at the Wentworth Arms Hotel in honour of our beloved
teacher.

In 1918, between my thirteenth and fourteenth birthdays, I grew seven
inches, much to everyone's amazement. I literally 'shot up' and, consequently, was a good example of the well-known description 'just skin and
bones.' That was my last growth in height, which brought me to five feet five
inches. I do not know what my weight was – certainly no more than 100
pounds, if that. Somewhere along the way I suffered from fever and pains,
mostly in the abdomen. The doctor described the condition as 'growing
pains,' and I have never yet had any other description, but I know that I was
unable to attend school for about two months. On the day I returned, Easter
exams began. I must have been reading a lot while I was ill because, despite
my absence, I received high marks.

Instead of going to Collegiate, which my family could not afford, I enrolled
in the Commercial program after graduating in 1918 from public school,
partly because I loved mathematics and partly because it was the shortest
route to full-time employment. Commercial was a three-year stint. Courses
were taken in a different school each year, and Commercial was always the
principal's class. In my first year of Commercial studies, I attended Central
School, where Mr Elmer Ward was the principal. Again, I had a contest for
first place. Grace having gone to Collegiate, my new class rival was Jean
Smith, who, like Grace, excelled in some subjects, while I made higher marks
in others. At the end of the year, book prizes were awarded. I received four
beautiful, leather-bound volumes. The first prize for Commercial work
earned me *Hypatia* by Charles Kingsley and *A Child's Garden of Verses* by
Robert Louis Stevenson. For the second prize in General Proficiency, I
received *The Ebb Tide* by Robert Louis Stevenson and *Rob Roy* by Sir Walter
Scott. *Hypatia* was probably my favourite. I often think of the words of Aben-

Ezra: 'People are apt to disdain what they know they cannot do.' The world is full of examples that bear out the truth of those words.

The second year of Commercial was in Ryerson, to which I was glad to return. The principal was Mr J.L. Stewart, a most kindly and dignified man. I admired him greatly and got to know him better in later years through my husband, Gordon, with whom he shared a common interest in the Scottish Rite. In my third year, I was in Queen Victoria School, which was a good two miles from home. Since a ride on the streetcar cost five cents (students' tickets were eight for a quarter), I walked more often than not. Mr Nichol, a large and rather terrifying man, was the principal there, and I was scared green of him. I sat in a seat in the very back row, and one day he paused by my chair as I was writing. Seizing my arm in a bruising grip, he said, 'That's no way to write,' and proceeded to instruct me in free hand – that is, from the shoulder. I have many times wished that I could have had an occasion to thank him (despite my bruised arm), particularly when I have seen others with 'writer's cramp' from writing with cramped fingers. I thought of him kindly also when, as a bookkeeper in a brokerage office during the market crash of 1929, I was writing constantly for fifteen hours a day. Over the years, I have frequently received positive comments on my handwriting, and I have Mr Nichol to thank.

Sundays were strictly observed in our household, and we children were raised on the Bible and regular attendance at Zion Methodist Church. The normal routine, for those of 'tender' years, was to attend Junior League, which was held at 10:00 a.m., followed by the service at 11:00. The service usually lasted about an hour and a half, after which we would walk home (about three-quarters of a mile), have a pick-up lunch, and return for Sunday School at 2:30. The afternoon was free after four o'clock, but there was no activity except reading, which was limited to the Bible, Sunday School papers, and other religious materials. We could also play the piano and sing but, again, just hymns and other religious music – no popular stuff! It would have been a very boring day had we not been so busy.

By the time I was fourteen, I was teaching Sunday School at Zion, first at the kindergarten level and later to increasingly older pupils. Eventually, I took on a class of young people studying to become teachers at the Normal School. Their subsequent successes in religious studies examinations earned me an unexpected letter of commendation from the Ontario Department of Education. I presume that my pupils reported their Sunday School classes because I was quite unaware that I was contributing to their religious studies at the Normal School.

During my adolescence, mother began to think that I was spending too much time at church events, but she must have realized that it was the result of our early training. It was also the place where friendships were made and courtships conducted. At one church-related social occasion held in a private home in 1921, I met Gordon Fairclough. We were both sixteen years old (he was younger than I, having been born in June and I in January). Although I had other suitors, and even an offer of marriage when I was seventeen from a business acquaintance of Rhea's husband, Gordon and I have remained together for nearly seventy-five years. Gordon had been brought up in the Anglican church, where his father served as a Sunday School Superintendent for more than twenty-five years. After our marriage, in January 1931, I was confirmed in the Anglican church and our son, Howard, was baptized at St George's Anglican.

The Anglican church in the interwar years was less strict than the Methodist in its approach to social activities, in which Gordon and I increasingly were becoming involved. On recalling our youth in Hamilton, Gordon remembered an incident that sheds some light on the severity of religious observance among all Protestant denominations in Hamilton. At one of our social gatherings, we had the bright idea of renting a hall, hiring an orchestra, and holding a dance which would be attractive to more than just our small group. Most houses could accommodate only about fifteen couples, and we had visions of a much larger event. When one of the elders in our church heard about the plan, he put his foot down and warned that if we went ahead with the proposal we would have to leave the church. The general opinion among the church elders at the time was that any public hall that permitted dances was a den of iniquity. It was thought that a private party held at home was always chaperoned by parents and therefore immune to the sins of smoking, drinking, and sex. Ha! Now these same churches are happy to have their young people hold dances in church halls and even encourage such social events. Today's scandal, it seems, is tomorrow's amusement, which should make the future, if there is one, rather interesting.

In the spring of 1921, at the age of sixteen, I graduated with my commercial diploma. Gordon had quit school after grade eight to join his father in the printing business, so when we met we were both making our own way in the world. In my case, it was important that I make a larger contribution to the family, which was once again caught in the tight squeeze of the hard times that followed in the wake of the First World War.

2

Girl of the New Day

My first paid work, during the Christmas season of 1917, was as a 'cash girl' in G.W. Robinson's department store, overlooking Gore Park, near the busy intersection of King and James. Since I was only twelve at the time, I had lied about my age, saying that I was fourteen, the minimum age for employment. It was my job to pick up the purchases and the cash from the sales clerk, and take them to the cashier who would wrap the items and deposit the money. I then carried the parcel and any change back to the sales clerk, who handed them to the customer. During the busy Christmas season the clerk would call 'cash' even before I had finished the previous assignment.

From then on I was never without a part-time job of some kind after school, on Saturdays, and during summer holidays. When I was fourteen I was employed as a sales clerk on Saturdays and school holidays by F.W. Woolworth, on King East. We worked from 8:30 a.m. to 10:00 p.m. on Saturdays. My father would be waiting to walk me home (about a mile and a quarter) after work. By that time the sidewalks in front of the store were crowded with young men waiting for their girlfriends. The boys made a practice of coming into the store to strike up a conversation with their favourite sales clerk in an effort to make a 'date' for after work. Since I looked older than my fourteen years, my father thought it wise to come for me himself.

The F.W. Woolworth Company can perhaps be thanked for the fact that I never took up smoking. On one occasion the store had a sale on prunes, and several of us were dispatched to the basement to pack them in one-pound lots. The basement was poorly ventilated, with inadequate lighting, so the ambience fell far short of being ideal. We worked with our hands, and the smell made me think of tobacco – the colour didn't help much either. Thereafter, whenever I thought of smoking, I remembered the nasty, smelly, sticky mass of prunes and could not put a cigarette to my mouth. Nor could I understand the girls of my own age who were sneaking behind doors to snatch a few puffs. In the 1920s smoking was considered a rather glamorous and certainly naughty thing for a girl to do, but I was immune to the temptation.

Since I was only sixteen when I made my entry into the full-time labour force in 1921, I was often tempted to lie about my age in order to be considered eligible for a better job. While searching for work, I applied for a position as a cashier-bookkeeper advertised by the Heintzman piano store on the corner of King and John streets. The interview went well, and the prospect of being hired seemed bright until I was asked my age. When I replied that I was sixteen, I was told that they required someone at least eighteen years old. From then on, I lied about my age to the extent that I actually forgot how old I really was and sometimes had to deduct the year of my birth from the current year in order to be accurate. Some time later, while I was working at K&S Rubber Company, the manager defended the shortcomings of an employee by saying, 'She is only nineteen,' to which I responded that I was also nineteen. 'Well,' he replied, 'that is what you told me your age was when you came here two years ago.' I, alas, was never a good liar. To be a good liar, you must have a good memory.

My first full-time job was as a stenographer with the Hamilton Soap Works. Hours were 8:30 a.m. to 5:00 p.m. during the week and 8:30 a.m. to 1:00 p.m. on Saturday, for which I was paid $8 a week. I lasted only a month because of a careless mistake. When the time came to make out the sales tax return for April, which had to be filed the end of May, I dated the period for reporting as ending on 31 April. I presume the manager suffered some ridicule in the government sales tax office, because he came back in a rage over this gross error and fired me on the spot.

I was thrown back on the job market in the 'bad' spring of 1921. The relief rolls were increasing rapidly, so I was able to find work as a stenotypist with the Hamilton Relief Office. The manager was Mr MacManamy, and his assistant was Miss Sarah Manderson, a most capable woman who was highly respected by the staff. Among the other employees, the one I recall most vividly was Archie Wright, an energetic young man who later went on to work with the Canadian National Railways. He was a very fast typist, but his main job was that of interviewing applicants for relief. This he did through a window between the office and the waiting room, and his conversations were frequently overheard. On one occasion Archie was interviewing an applicant whose English was rather weak. In answer to a question concerning the size of his family, he reported five sets of twins, to which Archie queried, 'What? Twins every time?' The applicant cheerfully responded, 'Oh, no – lottsa times, none at all.'

In the summer of 1921, unemployment in Hamilton reached such alarming proportions that a special department was established to dispense work permits to able-bodied men. To qualify for food vouchers the men were required to do manual labour on civic projects. It was a case of either work or be denied access to relief. Hordes descended on the new employment office (located in a large room on the second floor of what had once been a fire hall on Hughson Street), having been referred there by the Relief Office. Some had rather interesting reasons why they could not do manual labour. One individual claimed that he could not take a job because he was a musician and might damage his hands. On examination, his hands turned out to be gnarled and calloused, with very dirty finger nails. (Nice try!)

The hard times following the war brought our family economy close to peril. In 1922 I was the only member living at home who had a job, although mother continued to keep boarders, which brought in some much-needed cash. Even my boyfriend, Gordon, was the victim of the recession that held Hamilton in a tight grip. Gordon normally worked with his father at the printing plant, but during a brief lay-off due to lack of orders he took a job as a 'delivery boy.' Hyslop Brothers, a wholesale confectionery company, delivered its products in a Ford truck usually driven by Ross DeGrow. He was widely known for his ability to crank up the motor, step to one side, and jump behind the wheel of the truck as it went by. Ross must have been on holidays or otherwise indisposed, because Gordon took over this job for a short time and became as adept as Ross had been at 'jumping aboard' at just the right moment.

By the spring of 1922 economic conditions had improved sufficiently to enable the Relief Office to wind down its activities. I was laid off but immediately found work as a sales clerk at the Right House, a fashionable clothing store on King East, facing Gore Park. After the Easter season, that job, too, came to an end. I then took a position as stenographer in the law offices of Mewburn and Marshall. My boss was Stan Jefferess, who later became a good political friend, but I was less than enthusiastic about the position. I soon moved to the K&S Rubber Co. as clerk-stenographer at the then-quite-respectable sum of $17 for a five-and-a-half-day week. I owed this job to Pauline Mothersill, who also worked there and with whom I had become acquainted through our common membership in the Ladies' Basketball Association.

At this stage I did indeed play basketball – all 100 pounds of me. Although I was only five foot five, I was taller than many of the other girls and played centre. One time I had the wind knocked out of me when I was thumped by a 150-pound opponent. I was never a very good player, being light and generally not very well trained.

K&S's branch sales office served the Niagara Peninsula and as far west as London and its surrounding area. Owing to the popularity of the automobile, its tire sales were booming. In 1922 the tires on most automobiles were 30 by 3½ inches, with inner tubes. There was also an 'oversize' tire at 31 by 4 inches. K&S developed a tire that it called 'Supreme,' which had a row of vacuum cups down the middle of the tread. When in motion, particularly at high speed, it produced a distinct whistle. It was a popular tire, especially with the bootleggers, who drove large, high-speed cars (mostly Studebakers, if my memory serves me well). The regular tire carried a 4,000-mile warranty, while the Supreme was guaranteed for 8,000 miles. Nevertheless, the bootleggers would not trust their tires for anything like that length of use and came into K&S frequently for new sets of tires. Although they could outrun the police, who were on motorcycles, they could not take the chance of a flat tire on their trips to and from Montreal.

Much of Canada and the United States was sentenced to prohibition laws in the early 1920s, and bootlegging became one of the fastest-growing industries on the continent. During the two years that I worked at K&S I got to know quite a few 'practitioners.' One particularly handsome man by the name of Tony Valenti (the George Raft type) gave me a bottle of rye when he learned that I wanted one for my mother. Imagine his consternation when he found out that she applied it externally, mixed with camphor, for headaches! Most teenagers today would never admit to such a use of alcohol by their mothers, but I was, I fear, a rather naive adolescent.

Although I may have been naive, I was no slouch when it came to making money. To supplement my income from K&S, I used part of my noon-hour break to 'keep the books' for the Hamilton Machine Co. just a half-block away, on Ferguson Avenue. For the five afternoons, I was paid $4. This brought my income up to $21 a week, which was pretty good in those days.

Radio was the great communications breakthrough of the 1920s, and it was while working at K&S that I heard my first broadcasts. One of our shippers-cum-tire-repair-men, Ernie Graves, was a radio buff. He brought his 'crystal set' to work and, during lunch hour, set it up in the conference room, where we would all gather to see if Ernie could 'bring something in.' We got mostly squeals and hums, but occasionally his searching wire would hit a station, much to our delight. In early radio there were many informal and amusing announcers. The one I recall most vividly worked for WOW in Cincinnati, where he frequently announced his station as 'Cincinnati OO-HOO.'

I enjoyed K&S and was sorry when its Hamilton office closed in 1924. At the invitation of Ed Precious, I worked for a few months at Dunlop Tire, helping it straighten out its inventory, which was a mess. When that job came to an end, I moved on to the Carter Welding Company, which, in addition to the welding activity, had the franchise for Firestone Tires. I had a run-in with one of its auditors, who, I must say, was not a very nice man. Mr Carter's son, who managed the firm, helped me find my next employ-ment, as a secretary to the manager of the Bank of Nova Scotia. While this was a good position, I never really liked stenography.

My first love was bookkeeping and anything involving figures and calcula-tion, so I remained on the lookout for a job more 'up my alley.' In 1928 the big break came when I was offered a place in the office of the stockbroker W.H. Magill. The manager of the bank tried, without success, to get head office to meet the salary offered by Mr Magill. He should have saved him-self the bother. I would have left the bank in any event for the more attrac-tive opportunity. Of all the jobs I held in the 1920s, this was my favourite. I earned the princely sum of $100 a month, while learning the arcane myster-ies of one of North America's most glamorous professions.

When I went to work in the brokerage business, I was told that my wardrobe should reflect the professional image that the company wanted to convey. It was therefore necessary for me to give more thought to how I dressed. The best clothing store in Hamilton in the 1920s was Raphael-Mack. I had been acquainted with both Stan Raphael and Louis Mack, but it was the latter who took the most interest in my appearance. He was a very particular individual, and I could usually rely on his judgment. One day he greeted me with the words, 'I have just the dress for you.' When he showed it to me, I exclaimed, 'Louis, I can't wear black!' He said, 'Nonsense, every-one can wear black.' We each insisted upon our point of view until, finally, he persuaded me to try it on. When I emerged from the fitting room he exclaimed, 'Migod, you're right – take it off!' He never showed me a black or dark navy dress again.

Because of the heavy smoking by the clientele in our low-ceilinged boardroom, my clothes literally reeked of tobacco smoke. Consequently, I had to send clothes to the dry cleaners with alarming frequency. Dry clean-ing was a major investment, at $3.50 for a single item. It was not uncom-mon for my bill to reach $14.00 a month, which was a lot of money. The price of $3.50 seems to have been a popular one, because it was what we also had to pay for silk stockings. Because of their expense, they, too, required special care. If they developed a run, they could be repaired by shops that specialized in restoring them. Of course, silk stockings were not nearly as sheer as they later became and were nothing at all like the 'nylons' we could procure after the Second World War.

During the summer of 1928, I had the best part of every afternoon free. The stock market was usually sluggish during the summer months, and, in addition, the New York Stock Exchange was on Daylight Saving Time while Hamilton was on Eastern Standard. We had wires in the office to Toronto, Chicago, Montreal, and New York, but we were usually through the day's activities by 2:30, and we left when the day's work was done. During those free afternoons, my sister Mary, doing vocals, and I, accom-panying her on piano, became regular performers on the local radio station, CHML. The studio was located at the back of a store at 222 King Street East, from which the proprietor, George Adams, sold radios, stoves, and other appliances. He also acted as manager for the station and was des-perate to fill the listening void. Anyone who could make a reputable sound on the microphone was asked to 'go on the air.' I can recall, for instance, a rather nondescript character with a 'musical' saw and a violin bow being granted air time!

My brief foray into the wonderful world of radio did not, for good reasons, lead me into a lucrative recording contract. It did, however, bring me more work. In the course of my hanging around the studio, Mr Adams confided to me that his books were in 'one terrible mess.' This was in the early days of 'time' payments, and the system of drawing up contracts was not very sophisticated. The result was that he had no idea where he was financially, and apparently the people who were buying his contracts had little idea either. He had hired an accountant to straighten out the mess, but he got nowhere. I agreed to look at the situation to see what I could do. For the next few months, when I left the brokerage office I went immediately to Mr Adams's store, where I tried to unscramble the books. The work usually continued well into the evening. Perhaps I had more patience than the accountant, for I succeeded in bringing order to his accounts. Mr Adams was delighted.

My association with Mr Adams also led to my first airplane ride. An ex–air force pilot by the name of Don Urquhart was a member of the store's sales staff. On learning that I was interested, he offered to take me up in a plane at his disposal at the little airport on the eastern outskirts of Hamilton. It was a biplane, but I cannot describe it further except to say that the pilot occupied the rear seat and the passenger the front one. We communicated through the microphones in our helmets. Probably we did not fly very high, but I do recall that when we banked I felt that I could reach out and touch the ground. From that day on, I was hooked, and took every opportunity to fly. A few years later (when Howard was about three years old), a remote cousin of mine, Joyce Reid, took us up in a Piper Cub. My initiation in commercial flying was on the Trans-Canada Air Lines fourteen-passenger, and later twenty-one–passenger, planes, on which I flew a number of times.

As a working girl, I also continued my involvement in church-related activities. I can remember the long and serious discussions attendant on the union of the Methodist, Presbyterian, and Congregational churches in 1925. Zion joined the United Church, but there were many 'continuing Presbyterians.' Even before union, young people belonging to the three Protestant churches in our area enjoyed social occasions together. We joined forces for Young People's Society and amateur theatricals, and we had a great rivalry in basketball.

Our men's basketball team, under coach Stan Burnes, was famous for its spirited contests with teams from St George's Anglican and Erskine Presbyterian. On occasion, I confess, we provoked an atmosphere that fell somewhat short of Christian good sportsmanship, but it was great fun and healthy entertainment for the west end of Hamilton, and I never missed a game if I could help it. My interest in sports moved beyond its awakening in church basketball leagues. Later in life, I held administrative positions with both the Ladies' Basketball Association and the Hamilton and District Ladies' Softball Association. I am still an avid baseball fan, having got hooked on the Michigan-Ontario League, whose Hamilton games I watched from the third-storey windows in our family home on Tuckett Street. The teams played on what we called the 'cricket grounds,' more properly the HAAA ('H Triple-A') grounds, home to the Hamilton Tigers before their move to the Stadium.

I was a member of Zion's debating team, along with Cecil Robinson, who later became a lawyer and Queen's Counsel. From the time of his graduation until his death in 1988, Cecil was our lawyer, counsellor, and friend. When he and Kitty were married, I played the organ for their wedding. Cecil's sage advice saved us from unwise action more than once, and we always took his counsel seriously. He had a keen, if droll, sense of humour, which amused his friends and often took the edge off what might otherwise have been an acrimonious situation. I learned a great deal from him about both debating and the law that served me well in my public career.

Our Young People's Society also produced one three-act play each year in which I usually played a role. After performing on the Zion stage for several nights we would be invited to do performances in other church auditoriums and halls in Hamilton. The director was Bert Cook, a much-loved and respected leader of many activities in our church. Dramatic acting is to be highly recommended for the development of a stage presence and a carrying voice, both useful assets in any political career.

Activities associated with the church also served as an apprenticeship for other community organizations to which I eventually belonged. Drawing on our maternal heritage, Rhea, Mary, and I joined the United Empire Loyalist Association in the 1920s, when Stanley Mills was president of the Hamilton Branch. Although the Dominion Association was fraught with turbulence, the Hamilton Branch carried on evenly under the guidance of Mills, whose diplomacy resolved many disputes. Stanley Mills commissioned the now-famous statue of a Loyalist family, by Sydney March, which stands in front of the Court House in Hamilton and was featured on a Canadian stamp in 1934. When the expense of maintaining Dundurn Castle stirred a local movement for its demolition, he was instrumental in rescuing the stately home of Sir Allan MacNab, the one-time premier of the United Province of Canada who cobbled together the alliance that Sir John A. Macdonald turned into the Conservative Party. Because of Stanley's interest and considerable outlay of personal funds, the 'Castle,' at the spectacular northwestern approach to the city, has grown in beauty and in fame. It is now regarded as a jewel in Hamilton's crown.

In the Hamilton Branch of the United Empire Loyalist Association, a group of young people met frequently in the homes of other members. One of the members, Robert S. Johnston, subsequently served as Dominion President, and, in 1939, I became Secretary of the Dominion Association. More recently, the local branch has named me its Honorary Patron. In 1969 the Huguenot Society of Canada, which was founded in 1966, named me its Patron.

While still a teenager, I joined the Margaret Gage Burkholder Chapter of the Imperial Order Daughters of the Empire (IODE). The IODE had made a major contribution to the Canadian war effort through its voluntary activities and was at the pinnacle of its success. In Hamilton, it had a large following and was active in signing up young members. Pauline Mothersill, my predecessor at K&S and a fellow basketball enthusiast, recruited me. Like the Zonta, which I joined in later years, the IODE served as a training ground for my later foray into politics. Its officers insisted on following parliamentary procedure, and it was under their tutelage that I learned the intricacies of the Rules of Order. During the interwar years I moved steadily through the ranks to become a Regent, then a member of the Executive Board of the Provincial Chapter, Provincial Secretary, and Officer of the National Chapter.

There was a great deal of camaraderie among the executive members of the IODE, especially when the annual meeting was held at a distance. Several days on the train provided an opportunity for personal contacts and considerable frivolity, which might have surprised some members of the 'rank and file' who held their officers in high esteem!

Gordon was also a great 'joiner' and at the age of 23 became a member of the Scottish Rite, a Masonic fraternity that still plays an important role in our lives. In 1920 the Masons purchased the Tuckett family mansion (constructed in 1895 by the tobacco manufacturing magnate on the corner of King West and Queen) as the site of their Cathedral. The building was dedicated with great fanfare in 1923. Gordon subsequently achieved the highest rank in the Scottish Rite, the 33rd degree, which admits him to the Supreme Council, the governing body for all of Canada.

With Gordon's encouragement, I also joined the Conservative Party, for reasons that seemed logical at the time. In the interwar years the Liberals supported free trade, which, we felt, would have crippled the branch plants that brought so much prosperity to our city. The Conservatives were the champions of John A. Macdonald's high-tariff policy, one much better suited to what we thought were Canada's interests. Our political choices no doubt surprised our parents, since both the Cooks and the Fairgloughs were long-standing Liberals. My father regularly held forth on reciprocity, which he pronounced 'reeciprocity,' as many did. Mother reputedly voted the way my father told her to, but the secret ballot may have given her an opportunity for a minor rebellion against his dictatorial ways. Certainly, more than one voter was defying political loyalties in postwar Ontario. Gordon's mother, the former Annie Partridge, was a first cousin to E.C. Drury, leader of the United Farmers of Ontario and Premier of Ontario from 1919 to 1923. Of course, times change, and the younger generation does not always vote the way its parents did. Party platforms also change. Today, the Progressive Conservatives are supporting free trade and encouraging our huge manufacturing interests to compete with their American counterparts.

   In retrospect, I remember the 1920s as busy, happy years. I lived at home, had a boyfriend, worked at interesting jobs, and never seemed to have a dull moment. We went dancing at the Alexandra in Hamilton or to the Brant Inn in Burlington, and even drank a beer or two. In the summer of 1929 Gordon and I piled into the car with his parents for a holiday in New England. We stayed at tourist homes, visited all the sites, including Mount Washington, and enjoyed ourselves tremendously. By that time, I had a good Kodak camera (which I still have) and documented our trip in a photograph album that still sits on my living-room shelf as a testimony to those carefree days.

Then, in October 1929, came the Crash. As an employee of a brokerage firm, I was in the thick of the crisis and even lost my own savings as stock prices tumbled. The panic on Wall Street precipitated unprecedented activity, which our small staff was forced to handle. Before the age of computers, we did everything by hand. All transactions had to be recorded, books balanced, and margins calculated at the close of each trading day. At the depths of the crisis, the ticker-tape, received in brokers' offices, ran some two hours behind trading, so it was useless to the average trader in determining the current state of the market. We had to type all confirmations on manual machines to be mailed to clients or picked up by them immediately. In addition, we evaluated very active accounts for margin requirements several times a day and insisted that margin calls be covered on demand instead of the 'day after.' Failure to comply meant instant liquidation. Everyone worked at top speed. Even in offices that had more modern equipment (such as the 'Telex,' which was an improvement over the telegraph 'bug' we had to rely upon exclusively), this situation was common, and we heard reports of people in other brokerage offices collapsing and being hospitalized.

The pace certainly was gruelling. For one solid month, Mr Magill, the other two women employees, and I arrived at the office around 9:30 a.m. in preparation for the opening of the markets at 10:00. We never left the office before 1:00 a.m., Saturdays, Sundays, and holidays included. One day we worked right through to 5:00 a.m. I can remember Mr Magill marvelling that his 'girls' could stand it, especially me, a 'skinny little wretch' (Mr Magill's description) and younger than the others.

Although he worked us hard, Mr Magill and his wife took good care of us. We had no time to go out for lunch or dinner so Mrs Magill brought to the office a huge hamper of sandwiches and lots of coffee. These we would spread out on the desk in Mr Magill's office. When we had a few minutes we would grab a bite to eat, sometimes carrying our sandwiches and coffee back to our desks. There was never a night when he did not drive the three of us to his home after work for a biscuit and a drink. I did not drink much then, but he insisted on giving me a glass of Madeira – 'Methodist or no Methodist, you drink that,' he admonished – while the others downed something stronger. He would then drive us home so we could get a few hours of sleep before we returned to the office the next morning.

Gordon and I were engaged to be married, but we did not see much of each other during the hectic month following the Crash. Mr Magill obviously understood the strain this separation caused us. After the long days ended, and we had received our well-earned bonus, he had the three 'girls' to his home for dinner, and he announced that he had something he wished to play for me on the gramophone. I can still see him putting this thick Edison record on a beautiful instrument; when the sound came on, it was 'Lover Come Back to Me,' from a then-current Broadway musical. We all had a good laugh about it.

Despite all our hard work, Mr Magill, like so many other brokers, was forced to declare bankruptcy. The collapse of McDougall and Cowans in Montreal, through which Magill corresponded, brought about his own demise. It was a sad day when he phoned to tell me the news.

My change in employment status prompted another momentous decision. Gordon and I had dated each other for nearly ten years and were widely assumed to be 'a couple.' Marriage seemed the logical step to take, but as long as I held a good job it made little sense for me to 'retire' from the workforce, which is what most women did when they got married. The collapse of Magill's brokerage firm sealed my fate. Since neither my parents nor I had the money to sponsor a fancy wedding, Gordon and I were married in a simple ceremony at St Paul's Cathedral in Buffalo on my twenty-sixth birthday, 28 January 1931. We had no money for a honeymoon – although we could say that we saw Niagara Falls. Instead, we hurried back to Hamilton, where we faced the challenge of setting up housekeeping during the worst years of the Depression.

PART TWO
A Woman to Be Reckoned With

1931–1950

FOR MOST WOMEN of Ellen's generation, marriage brought a shift in focus from the public world of work and play to the private realm of family. But women's life choices were beginning to change under the pressures imposed by the new industrial order. Some women were deciding to stay longer in the workforce before they married, while more married women were returning to the labour force after their children had left the nest. Many women were also choosing to have fewer children. Although birth control was still illegal and was frowned on by the Roman Catholic church, many people saw it as the answer to the problem of having too many mouths to feed.

Hamilton was a major Canadian centre for the birth control movement. Notwithstanding the law, Dr Elizabeth Bagshaw ran a local clinic that dispensed contraceptive devices to women who needed them. As Ellen notes in this section, Bagshaw was one of a small number of professional women who were changing their own lives and who joined forces in voluntary organizations such as Zonta to bring their perspective to bear on issues of the day.

The Depression forced Ellen out of the labour force, but it soon drew her back in. The difficulties of raising a family on Gordon's steadily shrinking income from the family printing business prompted Ellen to return to work on a part-time basis shortly after their son, Howard, was born. Soon she decided to hire a housekeeper so that she could turn her full attention to her paid employment. Since jobs were scarce, married, middle-class women seeking to enter the labour force had little difficulty finding the help they needed at home. Only 4 per cent of married women were in the paid labour force in 1941, but the figure grew significantly in the final years of the Second World War and has climbed steadily ever since; over half of married women now hold paid employment. In short, Ellen helped to pioneer a trend that eventually engulfed a majority of Canadian women.

Ironically, the Depression had created a demand for the very services at which Ellen was most skilled: accounting. In 1921, the Certified General Accountants' Association had voted forty-three to three that 'it was not in the interest of the association to admit women.' Within a decade it had been forced to relax this restriction. By the 1930s, Shaw Colleges in Toronto had a widely respected correspondence program that prepared candidates for the General Accounting exam. Ellen saw her chance and took it. When she earned accreditation in 1935, she became one of a very few females in a male-dominated field. She carved a niche for herself in office services, which ultimately led to her appointment as Secretary for the Canadian Wholesale Grocers' Association.

With a little help from their immediate families and a lot of hard work, Ellen and Gordon Fairclough emerged from the 'dirty thirties' in better financial shape than most Canadians. Their middle-class status was confirmed by their location in the fashionable suburb of Westdale, their involvement in a wide range of voluntary organizations, and, with Gordon's enthusiastic support, Ellen's election to the executive of the Ontario Young Conservative Association. Following the declaration of war in 1939, Ellen and Gordon both became involved in war work, and their businesses flourished.

Ellen's high public profile and the support of the local Progressive Conservative Party boss, R.R. (Tony) Evans, helped her to get elected alderman in 1946. She had little difficulty retaining her seat in successive years. In 1949 she headed the city-wide election for Board of Control and hence became senior controller and deputy mayor. Ellen is characteristically modest in describing her municipal career. Although Hamilton had a good record in electing women to civic office, she could not have held her seat had she not proved her worth. Few Canadian women broke into public life in the two decades following the Second World War, and those who did rarely survived long in an environment that was at best barely tolerant of them.

Ellen worked hard to win the approval of the voters in her ward and soon discovered that she had what every successful politician needs: the common touch. Stung by the snobbish attitudes of the Hamilton elite, who she felt looked down on her for her humble origins, she courted the ordinary people who readily responded to her friendly smile, cheery wave, and direct approach. Ellen went out of her way to assist those who sought her counsel, attended the funerals of the high and the low, and was sensitive to the cultural diversity that increasingly characterized Hamilton's population. Even when faced with personal tragedies, some of which she describes here, Ellen was inclined to put the interest of others ahead of her own. Little wonder that she was soon being targeted for a larger political arena.

With Gordon and Howard, 1932

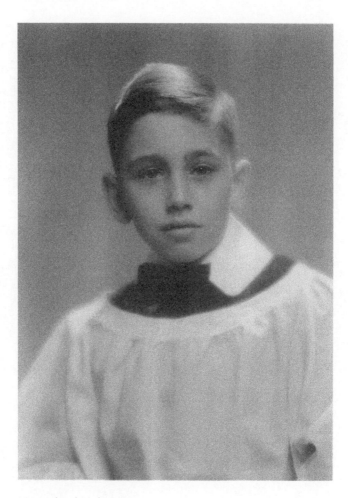

Howard in his choir gown

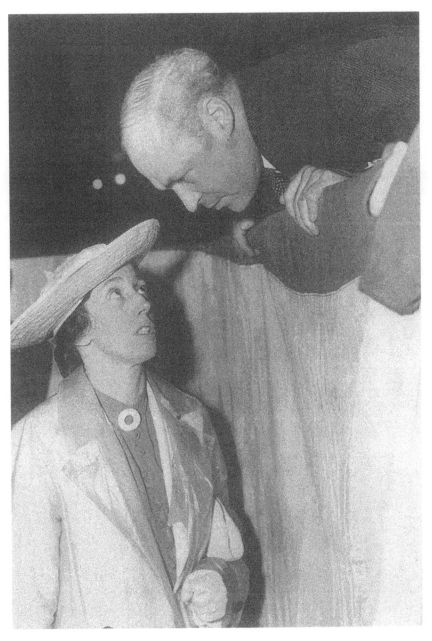

With Earl Rowe at the Conservative Party's national leadership convention, Ottawa, July 1938

'Conservative Lady Delegates' at the 1938 national convention

'Burnt sacrifices': Ash Douglas and I at the Ontario Conservative leadership
convention, December 1938. (Photo by the *Globe and Mail*)

United Empire Loyalist Association at Dundurn Castle, Hamilton, c. 1939

En route to an IODE Convention in Ottawa, October 1941.
(Photo by Trans-Canada Air Lines)

Zonta presents a jig-saw to the Occupational Therapy Centre in Hamilton, April 1942.

Relaxing with members of the Canadian Wholesale Grocers' Association, Chicago, January 1945

With Helen Anderson and Nora Frances Henderson, Hamilton City Council, June 1946

With Gordon and Howard, Vancouver, 1947. (Photo by the Vancouver *Sun*)

With Charlotte Whitton (left) and Ethel Brant Montour at a Zonta Conference in Hamilton, 1947

3

Double Days: Family and Career

In the 1930s, the dismal state of the economy made marriage a challenge for many Canadians. Jobs were scarce, and to be out of work often meant disaster, especially for men with families to support. Gordon and I soon learned that hard times were not just something that happened to other people. Within a year of being married, we were parents of a wonderful baby boy, short on income, and nearly out on the street.

Our first home was an upper duplex at 105 George Street in Hamilton. The owners occupied the main floor. While we had furnished the apartment quite adequately (Gordon sold his car to pay for the furniture), we had no money for frills, such as carpets for the hardwood floors. Howard was born in November 1931, and before the end of December we received notice to vacate the premises. Howard's cries, the noise of my heels on the hardwood floor, and my piano-playing were getting on our landlord's nerves.

With a month-old child and no transportation, we ran into real difficulties finding a place to live. My mother came to the rescue. She found an apartment at 286 Charlton Avenue, just a few blocks from my former home, at 12 Tuckett Street. We knew the two sisters who owned the place. Indeed, I had gone to school with their sister Grace Taylor, who had been one of my close competitors for academic honours. They were very kind to us, and we were most grateful not to find ourselves on the street in the winter of 1932.

Later in 1932 I got a call from George Adams, whose muddled accounts I had tackled three years before. He said that he was on the verge of going into receivership and that his books were again in a mess. According to him, his bookkeeper had neglected them rather woefully and then conveniently had a nervous breakdown. Would I come back and straighten things out? I told him that I could not do so because I had a small child who could not be left unattended. But Mr Adams had two girls sitting in his office 'twiddling their thumbs' because there was nothing for them to do. One of them was his own daughter Olive. Without consulting them, he volunteered their services. For about a month, Mr Adams sent one of 'his girls' each day to look after Howard and prepare our evening meal while I went to his office to unscramble his records to a condition acceptable to the receiver. I then returned to my domestic duties.

In early 1933, I received a telephone call from Allister Skinner, with whom I had worked in W.H. Magill's brokerage firm. He was then with another broker whose books needed urgent attention. It was difficult, he claimed, to find anyone familiar with the stock market who also had accountancy skills. He wanted me to come in, even if it were only in the evenings, to help straighten out the problems. With Gordon's income shrinking because of the worsening economic situation, I was glad to make some extra money. I started working evenings, which soon were stretching on to two and three o'clock in the morning. Since the broker also had a branch office in Kitchener, and sometimes traded through the office of J.H. Crang & Company in Toronto, travel out of town was frequent.

It was quite a struggle to maintain a home, look after a small child, and work such long evenings. I was also organist and choirmaster at a nearby church. Although I was paid $5 a month for my services there, it meant that even my Sundays were not really days of rest. Finally, my employers suggested that I put in full days and hire a housekeeper. I eagerly seized on this solution and soon found a willing candidate among the girls who sang in my church choir. Within a few months her mother decided that she wanted her back home, but there was no shortage of other women anxious to take her place.

At about this time, Isabel MacIsaac, who had once worked with George Adams, came to see me in great distress. She had been brought up by an aunt, her mother having died. Because her aunt had her own financial problems, she sent Isabel to live with relatives on a farm a few miles from town. Isabel had apparently found farm work too demanding and came back to the city, where she became a housekeeper for a clergyman's family.

There the days were long and the rules strict. She was required to be in every evening by ten o'clock and could go out only two nights a week. By the time she came to me, she was so distraught that she had little personal pride left. She readily admitted that she did not know how to cook – in her own words, she 'could hardly boil water.' Anyone who could read could cook, I said, if they used ordinary intelligence. Since she was a bright girl, she learned very quickly, and soon became a better-than-average cook. She remained with us for nearly eight years, making it possible for me to get on with my accounting career. When economic conditions improved during the Second World War, Isabel, who was trained in office work, decided to return to the business world. I secured a position for her with one of my clients, where she held for only a couple of years before she died tragically of cancer.

Despite the fact that Gordon and I were both working, we still had difficulties making ends meet. This time it was Gordon's mother who came to the rescue. In 1928 a new area of town, now part of Westdale, was surveyed west of Paradise Road and north of Main Street West. Gordon's mother was interested and convinced Gordon's father and us to visit the area. It was just a large, empty farm field with rough lanes and stakes stuck in the ground. Sensing a good investment, Mrs Fairclough purchased two lots on what became Sterling Avenue. Gordon bought a lot on Paisley Avenue North but was forced to sell it to his mother when the Crash left us in debt.

Mrs Fairclough subsequently had houses built on each of her Westdale properties, which she rented out. Although she eventually sold the Sterling Avenue properties, she kept the one on Paisley. Early in 1933 she suggested that we give up our apartment and move into her rental property because her current tenants were unsatisfactory. She offered us a good deal: we would pay the taxes plus a reasonable interest rate on her investment. We were most grateful to her and spent over six years at 50 Paisley Avenue North. In 1939 Gordon's mother died, and we moved into his old home at 214 George Street to take care of his ageing father, which we had promised his mother we would do.

Meanwhile, the situation at the brokerage office was becoming intolerable. Al Skinner had quit in disgust, and I felt obliged either to follow his example or to report my employer to the Securities Commission. In the end I decided to do both. There was some back salary owing to me when I left the firm, but I never expected to get it. Shortly thereafter, I received a call from Stanley Mills, who, with other members of his family, owned the Imperial Building at 25 Hughson Street South, just steps from King and James. I had known Mr Mills through our association in the United Empire Loyalist Association. There were several vacant offices in the building, and he suggested that I take an office on the ground floor, rent-free, and set myself up in practice, or, as he put it, 'hang out my shingle.' In return, I was to show offices to anyone interested in renting space.

It was a friendly gesture, but I had no furniture. So I went back to my former employer and said, 'Look, I propose to start up an accounting practice and I need furniture. Now you owe me some back salary and I would like to have it so I can furnish my office.' He had no cash but he did have furniture. If I would like to back up a truck to the door I could take what I needed. So I took a couple of desks, three or four chairs, and a battered old typewriter. I then went to Joe Hughes, who owned Hughes Typewriter, and whom I had known since my K&S days, when he was with Underwood. What could I do about this typewriter? He generously took it in trade and let me have a good, reconditioned machine on most lenient terms. Everyone was so kind.

Of course, in the 'dirty thirties' people helped out wherever they could. My first client was the Belgium Hosiery Shop, owned by Fanny and Jack Steinberg. I had been a customer of Fanny's before her marriage, when she had been the manager of a branch of Belgium Hosiery, and over the years we became good friends.

Since I was just getting started and had time on my hands, I enrolled in a correspondence course leading to accreditation as a General Accountant through Shaw Colleges of Toronto. Several more correspondence courses, supplemented by sessions in Toronto, ultimately led me to my goal. Later I applied for admission to the Certified Public Accountants' Association on the advice of Charles Walters, a leading Public Accountant who had been mayor of Hamilton and later Provincial Treasurer of Ontario. In 1953 the General Accountants' Association bestowed on me an Honorary Life Membership.

In 1935, Gordon's father bought out his partner in Heath and Fairclough, a printing firm founded by Alexander MacPherson in 1887. The Faircloughs had been involved in the firm since 1913, and it now became The Fairclough Printing Company Limited. The shop originally operated on James Street

North and later moved to 13 Charles Street. To my great surprise, Gordon told me that his father expected that I would move my offices to its premises so that I could run the administrative part of the business. I did so and lived with this arrangement until the early 1940s, when I moved to the third floor of 2 King Street West, which is now the main entrance to Jackson Square. In the intervening years my sister Mary had joined my staff. She remained to look after the Fairclough office and doubled her duties by working part-time for me at my new location. Her daughter, Joan, was attending commercial classes. Because of doubling up of school space during the war, she attended classes only in the mornings. In the afternoons she became an 'office girl' doing odd jobs and running messages.

Throughout my adult life, my sister Mary has always been there when I needed her. I really do not know what I would have done without her. While I was in Ottawa, she looked after my household bookkeeping. She invariably pitched in during election campaigns and was a great help in times of crisis. One time when I was in the cabinet, she even did my Christmas shopping!

Mary married Reginald C. Heels, an employee in the freight division of the Canadian National Railways, at about the same time that Gordon and I set up housekeeping. In the uncertain working conditions of the period, Reg was often 'bumped' from one position to another in the corporation. Their daughter, Joan Barbara, was born in Buffalo in 1932. A few years later they moved to Allandale, Ontario. When Mary found a job in a grocery store there, Joan came to live with us for a year. Joan and Howard, at about three and four years of age, respectively, were a great joy to us. As an adult, Joan has had a successful music career. She was employed as a Band and Choral Director with the Protestant School Board of Greater Montreal and later held a similar position in Hamilton.

Music has played an important role in both Gordon's and my families. It therefore should have come as no surprise that our dear son inherited an aptitude for music. But we soon realized that he had a very special gift. Even as a baby, Howard responded to music and was singing almost as soon as he could talk. He would sit on my lap while I played and sang to him, and very early on he would join in. He loved Christopher Robin songs and learned them all by heart. In contrast, he refused to sing Bad Sir Brian Botany. He knew which song was which by looking at the page, and when I came to

Bad Sir Brian, he would make a fuss until I turned the page to the next song.

At three years of age Howard had a very clear voice and perfect pitch. (I know some people will say this is unlikely, but it is true.) He loved to sing himself to sleep and knew all the popular songs of the day. He would start to sing as soon as we put him to bed. In the summertime, with the windows open, this three-year-old amused the neighbours with his favourite song, 'When I grow too old to dream.' At our church, All Saints Anglican, at King West and Queen, he always sat on the aisle, even at four and five years of age, so he could watch the choir procession. By the time he was six, he was pestering me to let him join the choir. I knew he was too young, but I told the Music Master, Eric Rollinson, who kindly suggested that I bring him for an audition, though he agreed he was too young. Eric had Howard sound several notes and sing a short hymn. Then he passed him the Prayer Book and asked him to read a passage, which he did. Eric looked at me and raised his eyebrows. 'Well,' he said, 'we don't usually take boys into the choir at that age because they cannot read. As a result they become restless, squirm about, and disrupt the proceedings. However, if you wish to bring him to choir practice after school on Friday, he may join the choir for the morning service.'

As soon as he could read, Howard started taking piano lessons. He studied with Jessie Gray, a fine musician and teacher. After a couple of years, she suggested that it might be better for him to study under Eric. This arrangement proved highly successful. By the time he was nine, he wanted to play the organ, and we had another consultation. Eric said that Howard's legs were not yet long enough, but he told him that he could study organ after he passed his next piano and theory exams. To me he confided that his feet would probably reach the pedals by then. In the meantime, he encouraged Howard to become familiar with the organ by going into the loft to tune the pipes. We soon discovered that he was walking on the pedals when he thought no one was observing. This early involvement bred in him a lasting love of the pipe organ, which he eventually came to play with great skill.

Over the years, Howard studied music under a number of talented teachers. Eric Rollinson left All Saints Church to take the post of music director at Grace Church On-the-Hill in Toronto. He then joined the staff of the Toronto Conservatory of Music, where he taught theory and organ. Unable himself to continue with Howard, Eric arranged for him to study

piano in Toronto under Weldon Kilburn. When Howard attended Westdale Collegiate, Ike Lomas, a member of a well-known musical family, was
in charge of the school's music department. Under Lomas, Howard won
the Junior League scholarship in music for two successive years, although it
was not normally awarded for a second time to the same person.

As a youngster Howard was one of only a few children in our social set
who had a working mother. When I returned to the business world in 1933,
it was unusual for a married woman to accept employment outside her
home (unless she did housework for other people), so I was looked at
askance by many friends and acquaintances. Even though we had Isabel
with us to keep house, I was actually snubbed by many people in the Westdale area where we moved in 1933. The majority of the residents were white-
collar workers with more pride than money, and the idea of a husband
'allowing' his wife to be gainfully employed was more than they could take.
Gordon let such comments roll off his back and encouraged me in my
career endeavours.

Howard also adjusted to having an unconventional mother. Many of the
youngsters who went to school with him made a habit of coming after
school to our house, where Isabel would feed them cookies and milk. Isabel
was undoubtedly at home more consistently than many mothers, a point
not lost on Howard and his friends. One day Howard was stopped on the
street by a woman who exclaimed, 'Oh, you poor little boy – I don't suppose you see your mother very often,' to which he replied with all the sin-
cerity of a six-year-old, 'I do too – my mother doesn't play bridge.' He told
us this story at home and was quite childishly indignant.

After Isabel left us we were fortunate to secure housekeepers – most of
them excellent. We also experienced our share of problems. In one case, the
woman's idea of a perfect day was to start with a quarrel. She would find
something to harp upon until we were all in a state of agitation. One morning she accused Howard of stealing the house key from her purse. It was a
ridiculous accusation, since Howard had his own key. She kept this theme
running, with her voice rising, until I lost my temper. People sometimes say
they are so angry they 'see red,' and that day I knew what they meant. I literally saw this woman through a haze of red before my eyes. In fact, I have
quite a bad temper, but I had kept it under control for some fifteen years.
After I had spoken my mind, I left the kitchen and went back to breakfast,
but I was shaking so badly that I could not hold the coffee cup. Howard put

his arms around me to comfort me before leaving for school, but I knew what had to be done. I went to the office and asked Gordon to go home and fire her. I suggested that he take Mary along as a witness. When they told her that her services were no longer required, she feigned astonishment and said that there had been a few words but that she had thought nothing of it. They stayed until she packed her things and then took her to the bus station. When we cleaned her room we found her key between some blankets on a chair.

In the aftermath of that confrontation, I was physically ill. The doctor kept an eye on my condition for three or four days and gave me some medication to help me 'cool down.' It was a real lesson, and I have never since permitted myself to become excessively annoyed, even in very trying circumstances.

One of our finest housekeepers was a Scottish woman by the name of Elizabeth Jevon. Despite a heart condition, she flew about her duties. She was a real prize. One of my clients was Wilf Easun, a stockbroker from Kitchener, who visited us when in Hamilton. He was quite a pipe smoker and left ashes in several trays. After he left Betty would say, 'Thot mon was here again.' Wilf was of Scottish origin, so when he next called, I made a point of taking him to the kitchen to introduce him to Betty, who was impressed that he shared her ethnic background. We never heard another remark about 'thot mon.'

One Sunday evening after I had become a Member of Parliament, I took the train to Ottawa as usual. During the night Gordon heard Betty moving around. In the morning she was not down to prepare his breakfast, which he thought odd, but be decided that she had slept in as the result of a restless night. After about an hour at work, he had second thoughts and persuaded Mary to go to the house with him to investigate. They discovered that she had died during the night. It frightened Mary to the extent that she still has vivid memories of that occasion. We were all very sad because Betty was a fine woman and only in her early sixties when she passed away.

My status as a business woman resulted in my joining the Zonta Club of Hamilton in 1937. A world-wide service organization founded in Buffalo in 1919, Zonta is composed of professional and executive women. I enjoyed my work with Zonta perhaps more than that with any other voluntary organization. Through Zonta I established friendships with distinguished women from many different countries and served as an officer at various levels, including President of the Hamilton Club, 1940–2, District Governor, 1948–9, and International Treasurer, 1972–6.

The first president of our Zonta branch in Hamilton was Jean McBride, who was the first practising female Public Accountant in Hamilton. Dr Elizabeth Bagshaw, famous for her pioneering activities in the field of birth control, joined the Hamilton branch of Zonta the same year I did. When she reached her 100th birthday in 1981, we organized a party for her. She did not long survive this milestone, but her friends will long remember her ready wit and quick smile, which endeared her to all – even those who opposed her efforts on behalf of planned parenthood.

In 1938 Zonta International established the Zonta Amelia Earhart Fellowship Awards in memory of the famous aviator who had been a member of Zonta in Boston and New York. When she disappeared in an apparent airplane accident in 1937, Zontonians decided to honour her by making awards to qualified women for graduate study in aerospace-related science and engineering.

By the late 1930s I was also active on the executives of the United Empire Loyalist Association, the IODE, and the National Conservative Party. My involvement in these groups helped to develop my deep respect and admiration for the selfless devotion exhibited by thousands of 'volunteers.' Without their help, many worthwhile projects would never get off the ground.

In 1923, when Gordon and I were eighteen years old, we became very interested in politics. It was an election year in Ontario, and, other than prohibition, the main issue was free trade with the United States. I can remember walking down Locke Street discussing the matter and coming to the conclusion that our city needed tariff protection for its industries, many of which were branch plants of American companies. This was the position taken by the Conservatives, led by Howard Ferguson, who defeated Premier Drury's Farmer-Labour government in July of that year.

We felt strongly enough about the issue to join the Junior Conservative Club as a prelude to becoming members of the Conservative Party when we were old enough to vote. When a Young Conservatives organization was later formed in Hamilton as a means of attracting both women and men under thirty-five years of age to active involvement in the party, Robert Marshall became the first President, and I followed him in that office. In the late 1930s I served as Vice-President of the Young Conservatives of Ontario. From these administrative positions I kept a close watch on the political scene both provincially and federally.

The provincial leadership convention was held at the Royal York Hotel in Toronto in May 1936, and Gordon and I attended. George Henry, Howard Ferguson's successor as premier and party leader, had been defeated by the Liberals under Mitch Hepburn in June 1934, leaving the party divided and demoralized. In a fiercely contested race, Earl Rowe, a farmer, stockbreeder, and MP for Dufferin-Simcoe, beat his nearest rival, George Drew, for the top job. But it was not the last we would hear from Drew. Although he ostensibly supported Rowe, he had a sudden change of heart and ran as an independent candidate in the 1937 election. I thought very highly of Earl Rowe (who subsequently became a client of my firm and a close personal friend) and was appalled by Drew's lack of loyalty. It would be many years before I could bring myself to forgive him.

Rowe lost the 1937 provincial election and resigned as party leader shortly thereafter to return to federal politics. When a convention was called in December 1938 to replace Rowe, I was front and centre in efforts to 'stop Drew.' J. Earl Lawson, a lawyer from Toronto and Member of Parliament for York South, was persuaded to enter the leadership race. He asked me to second his nomination, which was moved by Ash Douglas, from London. Of course, I was pleased and honoured to do so, but I have never forgotten Ash's remarks to me after we had signed the nomination paper. 'You know, Ellen,' he said, 'you and I are just a pair of god-damned burnt sacrifices.' And he was right. Although Drew and I became good friends in later years, I was not his favourite person during the years when he led the Conservative Party in Ontario.

While we lived in Westdale, we were in the federal constituency of Wentworth, a riding held by Conservative Frank Lennard from 1935. I was active in Frank's campaign and was chosen to attend the federal leadership convention held in Ottawa in July 1938 following the resignation of R.B. Bennett. John Robinson, a lawyer and later a judge, was another local delegate. His wife, Helen, accompanied him to Ottawa. Since Frank had accommodation at Lansdowne Park, he made his room in the Chateau Laurier Hotel available to Helen and me.

That was quite a convention. One night a group of young delegates went to Bowles Lunch, across from the Chateau, for a snack and got into an argument as to which candidate we should support. The discussion lasted all night, and I finally got back to my room at six o'clock in the morning. When I entered the room Helen opened a sleepy eye and said, 'You must be out of your mind.' She was probably right.

Because I was well known to the Hamilton West delegates, they invited me to sit in on their meetings. In that constituency, R.R. (Tony) Evans, QC, was the undisputed boss. He was a prominent lawyer and a political czar of no mean proportions. During one discussion in Tony's suite, he instructed his delegates on how to vote, and, typically, they all agreed with him. I was not so easily convinced. When I said, 'No, I can't vote for him because I don't approve of him or his tactics,' a gasp went up in the room. 'Imagine anyone defying Tony,' was the general attitude. Until that time I had had a very casual acquaintance with 'Mr Evans' – so much so that we were not even on a first-name basis. As we left his room, he walked out with me, put his arm around my shoulders, and said, 'Ellen, we don't see enough of each other.' He apparently liked being 'talked back to' by a young upstart. That incident was the beginning of a long and valued friendship, one fraught with great significance for my political career.

The incident I recall above all else during the 1938 convention was the magnificent speech that Arthur Meighen made to the delegates in support of a united Commonwealth defence policy. Meighen goes down in history as a rather crisp individual with great mental capacity but no ability to develop rapport with the average person. But there is no doubt that he was a great orator. His speech on opening day brought everybody to their feet, with the exception of the French bloc, which could never forgive him for his stand on conscription during the First World War. When I looked around, some of the men near me had tears rolling down their cheeks, they were so moved by his words and delivery.

Like the majority of delegates, I had great hopes that our new leader, Robert Manion, would appeal to the electorate, but he proved no match for the Liberals, who walked all over us in the 1940 federal campaign. By that time the war had changed a lot of things, including my business prospects.

Economic conditions in Hamilton picked up considerably with the outbreak of the Second World War, and my accounting practice grew accordingly. One client in particular expanded my professional horizons. Soon after the move to 2 King Street West, Samuel Vila, Secretary of the Canadian Wholesale Grocers' Association, asked if he could have desk space and secretarial service from my office. It came as a welcome suggestion. He used my office as a mailing address for the Canadian Wholesale Grocers, and soon I was opening his mail and answering a large part of it for him. The establishment of the Wartime Prices and Trade Board necessitated increased travel to Ottawa for Mr Vila, who was getting advanced in age and did not like that prospect at all. When he took ill, I carried on unofficially until he recovered. Eventually he reached a stage where he could no longer continue to work, and I was summoned to Toronto to discuss the matter with Mr McNally, the President of Canadian Wholesale Grocers. He invited me to take the post of Secretary to the Association. At first I demurred, saying that I was trying to build a practice, but he asked, 'Well, what would you have to do?' I would have to hire another person for my office, I replied. 'Well, go ahead and do it!' – which I did.

That was in 1940, and from then until 1954 I held the post of Secretary to the Canadian Wholesale Grocers' Association. I continued my accounting practice and also became involved in civic and national politics. It was a busy and exciting period of my life. My work with the Grocers' Association included travel to Ottawa, where I met departmental officials and Members of Parliament. When I did eventually get elected to the House of Commons, I was already familiar with the Ottawa scene and so it was not a strange entry for me, as it often was for so many new members.

The Grocers' Association meetings invariably included good times as well as hard work. I even earned an unusual nickname. We met in Toronto after the war to discuss surplus inventories of various kinds with a representative from the War Assets Corporation. During the meeting, Mr L.H. McGugan from London slid a note over to me which said, 'Why do you drink so much water?' I was not the only one drinking a lot of water that morning; nevertheless, I scribbled a reply that read, 'Because I'm made of dust, I guess.' The meeting proceeded, and when Mr C.H. Sly, the President of the Association, asked if there was any further business, McGugan piped up and said, 'Yes, I have a communication I would like to read.' Our short correspondence caused a big laugh around the table. Jim Sinclair, from Winnipeg, who was sitting at the far end of the table, said, 'Hi, Dusty!' and the nickname stuck. Whenever I am hailed in an airport or other public place with 'Hey, Dusty!' I know right away it is someone in the grocery business. The only other nickname I ever had was 'Cookie' – the logical consequence of my maiden name, Cook.

During the Board meeting of the Grocers in Winnipeg in 1945 there was a provincial election campaign being held in Ontario. Some of us were in the dining-room of the Queen Alexandra Hotel on the Sunday evening prior to polling day. John Bracken, the leader of the federal Progressive Conservative Party since 1942, was also dining there. We had met during the leadership convention in which I supported his candidacy, and when he spied me he came over to say hello. After he left, I took a great deal of ribbing because some of the Board members at our table were staunch Liberals. The discussion quickly turned to the Ontario election. Mr McGugan, who was a Liberal, wanted to bet me $5 that the Progressive Conservatives under George Drew could not form a government. I accepted the bet, and soon others were wagering on the number of seats the Conservatives would win. It began to get beyond me financially, but Walter Dilworth of York Trading, who was sitting on my right, whispered to me to take all the bets I could get and he would split them with me. This I proceeded to do. When the number rose to more than 50 seats I said, 'Oh no, I want odds on a bet of that proportion,' but I remained adamant that Drew would get that many seats.

The next evening we gathered in Kelly Douglas's suite to listen to the news, which early on indicated a healthy majority for the Conservatives. As the number of seats moved beyond the point of each bet (the Conservatives eventually took 66 seats), I received another $5 bill, to loud groans from Liberal supporters. At some point in the evening Michael Dwyer from Halifax shouted, to much merriment, 'You should change her name to 'Not-so-Dusty.'

During one meeting I was asked to take a long-distance call from home. Of course, one always anticipates trouble when receiving such a message, and I was quite concerned. It turned out to be from Howard, who had been followed home by a puppy. He wanted to know if he could keep him. If the rightful owner was not found and if his father approved, I replied, it would be all right. Although the foundling did not last long as the family pet, we eventually bought a beautiful Labrador retriever who answered to the name of Omar.

For several years, as part of my involvement in the Wholesale Grocers' Association, I attended the Boston Conference on Distribution, a joint venture of the Boston Chamber of Commerce and the Harvard School of Business Administration. It was a no-frills meeting, featuring a broad range of speakers on many different subjects. Presentations were strictly limited to twenty minutes. Given speakers as well at the two luncheons, we would hear over twenty presentations in two days. It was a highly academic affair and very stimulating. On two occasions, I had the honour of addressing the conference, and I was a member of its International Advisory Council for several years. In 1958, after I had become a member of the cabinet, I received a citation and was admitted to the Distribution Hall of Fame.

When I first ran for Parliament, in 1949, I wrote to all the Directors of the Canadian Wholesale Grocers' Association informing them that I proposed 'to throw my hat in the ring' and offering to submit my resignation. Some time earlier, during a Board meeting in Toronto, the feather in my hat had flicked annoyingly across Jim Sinclair's forehead when a bunch of us were crowded into a restaurant booth. I was therefore amused but not surprised when I received a sarcastic note from Jim, saying that there was no need to resign but that if I were going to throw my hat in the ring he hoped it was 'the g.d. thing with the feather in it.'

After I moved my practice to the third floor of 2 King Street West, I sublet some of the offices there and offered tenants optional stenographic services. The offices were occupied by various people, many of them engaged in sales, which meant that they were travelling most of the week. One day a young woman came into my office looking for space to establish a stenographic service. She temporarily based her operations out of my offices until she could find something more suitable, which she eventually did. While she was with me, her first clients were my own tenants, and when she moved to her new premises she took one of my tenants with her. I eventually forgot all about her until one day Al Skinner came to my office and asked if I was interested in buying a business. He explained that he and two associates, Cameron MacGillivray, Chartered Accountant, and Sam Manson, a well-known local sportsman and merchant, were planning to purchase a business, and if I could raise $1000 they would like me to join them. Since they were friends of mine, I acquiesced. However, I was dumbfounded to discover that the enterprise they proposed to buy was the office service that this young woman had started out of my premises only a couple of years earlier. Her grandiose ideas and poor business judgment had landed her deeply in debt, and she had dragged her partner, and my former tenant, down with her. The partner was a friend of Cam MacGillivray, who had spearheaded the proposal to buy out her bankrupt firm. We four incorporated as Hamilton Office Services Limited and picked up the pieces. Eventually, Cam's partner, Elmer Chagnon, who was also a Chartered Accountant, purchased a portion of the shares belonging to Cam and Al so that Sam and I each owned one-quarter of the investment and the other three each owned one-sixth. We all had known each other for many years, which perhaps accounts for the fact that our association was, for me, one of the most pleasant of my business life.

We engaged a very capable woman, Edith McCombs, as manager. For many years she had been the office manager for B.R. Marsales, who owned Soper's Tents and Awnings. Al Skinner undertook to oversee the operations on behalf of the owners. It was an admirable arrangement, and the business prospered. When Elmer Chagnon died, his wife, Jesse, became a member of our Board. We made a respectable profit when the business sold, thanks to Al Skinner's good judgment in investments.

This is not the end of the story, however. During the 1953 election campaign, my headquarters was in the old Spectator Building on James Street South. One day a gentleman came into the office and asked if he could speak to me privately. He had a shocking story to tell. It appeared that he had lent money to the young woman who had started Hamilton Office Services, and she was again too deeply in debt to pay off the loan. She had had the gall to advise him to call on me to reimburse him; in her words as reported by him, 'She is in the midst of an election campaign and cannot refuse.' The man wanted no part of it himself, but he thought I should know that she was up to such shenanigans.

At 6:00 a.m. on 3 January 1946, my brother Howard, who was with Bell Telephone, called to tell me that the building in which my office was located was on fire. I imagined all sorts of horrors. Although the firemen were wonderful, covering everything with tarpaulins, the heat and smoke caused damage to the typewriters and furniture, and it was impossible to work until the contractors were finished cleaning up the mess. Fortunately I was covered by insurance, which included even the cost of transporting members of staff from the office to their homes, where they worked during the day. We managed to survive the ordeal, but it was a particularly difficult time, with year-end deadlines to be met in the midst of all the chaos.

At this point, Gordon came home with the news that Dr Barney

Marsales, an osteopath, was renovating the basement area of his building at 152 James Street South. I jumped at the chance to occupy premises where both the rent and the taxes would be considerably less than what I was paying for prime property at King and James. My new location was just a few steps below street level. Like Christopher Robin, we were 'neither up nor down' but halfway in between. With windows and entrances at both front and rear, we did not have the feeling of being in the basement. One of the great advantages of our location, being in a row of attached stone premises, was that we enjoyed cool conditions even on the hottest days in summer. Occasionally a client would drop in just to cool off.

I occupied the James Street premises until I sold my practice in 1957. Accounting was, at that time, deemed to be a conflicting interest for a member of the cabinet. Fortunately for me, my friend Cam MacGillivray agreed to purchase my practice, which after my seven years as a Member of Parliament was, alas, not as prosperous as in the immediate postwar years. It was not until I was defeated in 1963 that I got 'back to business.'

In the course of my business career I had also become adept at raising funds for organizations, including the Progressive Conservative Party. One day I called on a well-known industrialist to solicit a political contribution, only to get the line that he had contributed repeatedly and frequently in recent years. He even called on his secretary to bring the record of his contributions. I said to him, 'Oh well, never mind. I don't want your money. You just agree to let your name stand for nomination instead.' He gasped and ordered his secretary to prepare the cheque for his signature!

At one point in my business career I was approached by a friend to see if I could use some office help. He was friends with a family who had a beautiful daughter – in fact, she was so beautiful that she could not hold a job because the male workers at any establishment where she was employed made life miserable for her with their unwanted attentions. He thought the solution would be for her to secure a position with a female boss, and I agreed to give it a try. Lilyen Toolivetro turned out to be a delightful young woman, as good-natured as she was beautiful. The only trouble was that she took twice as long as anyone else to do errands. It was not her fault. Wherever she went she was the object of attention, especially from men trying to date her. One day I returned to my office from an appointment to find the whole street agog. People were standing in doorways and leaning out of windows to discover the source of the hubbub. It turned out that a truckload of men from the *Hamilton Star* had seen Lilyen on their way to the liquor store. When I entered the office, everyone was laughing except Lilyen, who was embarrassed by the catcalls and wolf-whistles. Soon after this incident, Lilyen married Randy Atherton, an American serviceman. When he left the service, they moved to Rochester, where he took a position as a hotel manager. It was not long before Lilyen was a photographic model for Eastman Kodak Company. A few years later her little daughter also became a model for Kodak.

Lilyen's departure from my office was not my last association with the Toolivetro family. Her sister, Margaret, was employed in my office both before and after her marriage to Norman Green, and their mother, who was a wonderful designer and dressmaker, made clothes for me when I sat in Parliament. I was particularly fond of her creations from Indian saris, which she draped to simulate the styles worn by Indian women. When I wore them to dinners at the Indian High Commission the women would gather around me, intrigued by the excellent imitation of their style of dress. For my part, I wish that I could learn to drape a sari like Indian women do without it falling off!

4

Days and Nights in Civic Politics

During the war, a group of local men did war work 'off the record,' and Tony Evans, Tory 'boss' in Hamilton West, was one of them. He asked me if I would keep their records and generally act as liaison, to which request I agreed as part of my contribution to the war effort. He then said, 'You know I wouldn't have asked you if I could have found a man to do it.' What a back-handed compliment! Nevertheless, in choosing me for the job, he demonstrated his confidence in my discretion, because strict confidentiality was required. Gordon was on one of the teams whose members kept an eye on buildings in the city that might be subject to sabotage by enemy agents – a fact that I gleaned from the records I was keeping – but he did not mention it to me, nor did he know that I was working in a managerial capacity in the same organization.

On a number of occasions I have been given information with the admonition that 'this is in the strictest confidence,' and I always took such confidences seriously. Several times, the person who had offered me confidential information would visit us and begin talking about the subject in question in front of Gordon, who would immediately show his bewilderment. I would have to intervene to say that I considered the information to be 'strictly confidential,' to which the visitor invariably replied, 'Oh, yes, but I presumed that you would tell Gordon.' When is a confidence not a confidence? I am also very leery of gossip that is relayed to me or of any stories that have a derogatory slant. What does the teller of such tales say about me to another listener?

Tony did not request; he demanded! So it was that he telephoned me one day in 1945 and told me bluntly, 'Get over here – I want to talk to you.' That was his way, and I did not question him this time. He was alderman for Ward 3, and, as soon as I was seated, he told me that he did not intend to run for another term (one year in those days) because of the increased demands of his law practice. He then announced, 'You are going to run,' to which I replied, 'I certainly am not!' Instead of answering me, he picked up the telephone and called Gordon. 'Gordon,' he said, 'I have just told Ellen that I am not going to run for alderman again and that she is going to run in my place.' Gordon replied something to the effect that he thought this a great idea, and that was that. Of course, I could have stubbornly resisted the 'call,' but I was actually quite intrigued by the possibility of a political career.

Tony informed me that he and several other men would give me whatever support they could – short of financial. Since it had been rumoured that Bob Morrison, another Conservative and son of a former mayor of Hamilton, might run, I ventured that it would be foolish for both of us to run, because we might split the vote. Tony conferred with Bob's father, Bill, who told him that Bob would not be running. On the strength of this information I announced my candidacy, which was covered in a Saturday edition of the *Spectator*. On Monday, the same newspaper carried the announcement that Bob would also run.

It was a memorable campaign for me. I was nominated by Charles Ralph, a local businessman, and my friend Irene Dorsey seconded the nomination. Irene and my sister Mary worked tirelessly on my behalf. With Tony sitting beside the telephone at our house, we received the final results: I had lost by three votes! I spent the next month receiving regrets and excuses – someone had been ill, they had had to go to Toronto, and so on. Even if half of them had cast their ballots I would have won by a wide margin. No one can ever tell me that a single vote does not count! As it turned out, I served the term on Council despite my failure at the polls. A few weeks following the election Lance Smye, the other alderman in Ward 3, took a position as Hydro Commissioner and resigned as alderman. Instead of holding another election to fill the vacancy, Council offered me Smye's seat.

Besides Tony Evans's backing, my success in civic elections was due to a number of factors. Following the poor turnout in the 1943 civic elections –

only 19 per cent – I had been involved in a 'Get out the Vote' campaign. Irene Dorsey, Katherine McAuley, Mary, and I were ringleaders of this effort. Although we had no funds, we made our plans and enlisted the help of interested citizens, both women and men. One of our first targets was Bill Cranston, who was manager of radio station CKOC. He was a public-spirited citizen and proved instrumental in getting media cooperation during the 1944 civic elections. The result, a 40 per cent turnout, made it well worth our while. I have no doubt that my participation in the campaign contributed in some measure to the support I received at the polls in 1945 and subsequent years.

Although Tony was a powerhouse in Hamilton's political life, women's organizational networks also exerted considerable influence. Both Irene Dorsey and Katherine McAuley were involved in Home and School Association activities. Katherine was, for many years, a School Trustee and subsequently became Chairman of the Hamilton Board of Education. Irene was active in the IODE. When I took my seat on City Council I was Provincial Secretary and Vice-President of the IODE and Dominion Secretary of the United Empire Loyalist Association; I was Past President of the Zonta Club of Hamilton and chaired Region A, District 3, of Zonta International, which included American states as well as Canadian provinces. These organizations gave me and other women involved in them valuable contacts and good experience for political life.

During the war, women, of necessity, had become more active in public affairs, and I knew from my own experience that there was no looking back. I made it my business to talk to women about what I considered to be their duty to the nation that offered them so many privileges. In my capacity as a member of various voluntary organizations, I was often asked to speak to groups throughout Ontario. My argument usually went something along the lines of what I said to the annual banquet of the four Lakehead branches of the IODE, as reported in the *Fort William Daily News*, 8 June 1943:

When we look to the future we wonder what it holds for us. Demobilization is one great thing, especially for women in the services and industry, many of whom will be loath to go back to their old way of living. Another problem is the rearing of children in suitable surroundings – we must clear the slums and tenements and have homes where a child can enjoy comfort. ...

Women's place in the building of a great nation is increasingly important. ... Why in these days of cooperation, are there no women in the legislature? Are women so insignificant that they have no desire to be heard? If women were in the legislature a lot of things that are dirty would be cleaned up, they wouldn't stand for them. Before we can achieve anything we must build up self confidence, forget petty annoyances, and we have to select our leaders and then support them with courage and loyalty. Let us profit by our mistakes but let us relegate them to the past, it is the future that counts. Above all we must lend our courage and trust in a mass confidence in our ability to achieve; we have to work together with all kinds of people, in all kinds of conditions, with men and women alike.

Although Hamilton had never supported a woman for a provincial or federal seat, the city had a good track record of electing women to civic office. Nora Frances Henderson was the first woman to be elected to Council, serving as alderman from 1932 to 1935 and then as controller and deputy mayor from 1935 to 1947. Agnes Sharpe was alderman from 1935 to 1939, when, on returning from a trip to England on the *Athenia*, she was a victim of the first bombing of a passenger liner during the Second World War. In 1945 Helen Anderson, a Communist, was elected alderman, and she served two terms.

When I went on Council in June 1946, Samuel Lawrence, a dedicated supporter of labour and the Co-operative Commonwealth Federation (CCF), was mayor. Although I was of an entirely different political stripe, I found him to be an honest and courageous individual. Lloyd Jackson, a highly successful businessman, was elected mayor in 1949. Jackson was a Liberal politically, and, although we did not always see eye to eye, I respected his ability to get things done.

During the years I served on the Council, the population of Hamilton was under 200,000 – half of what it is today. Civic elections were held every year until 1954, when a two-year term was introduced. Taxes were relatively low, and so, too, were salaries. As aldermen we received the princely sum of $400 a year.

My first few months on Council were busy ones. The workers at the Steel Company of Canada (Stelco) and several other industries were on strike, and Mayor Lawrence was reluctant to take strong action against them. Nora Henderson was made of sterner stuff. When it looked as if the strikers had taken complete control of the situation, she bravely marched through the Stelco picket lines to demonstrate that she could go where she pleased within the law. Nora left civic politics in 1947 to become Secretary of the Children's Aid Societies of Ontario. Her untimely death two years later from cancer was a great loss to Hamilton.

Early in my civic career, a proposal to widen Main Street West came before Council. A bottleneck had developed west of Queen because the street narrowed from four to two lanes at that juncture. The widening, of course, would take a slice of property off the front lawns on Main Street from Queen Street westward. In some cases, it even took off verandas or required the relocation of the steps to the front door. The proposal created a great furor. Those who lived on the street were terribly annoyed, particularly with me, because I was their alderman. However, I felt that with the increase in vehicular traffic following the war, the road work simply had to be done.

I refused to give in to my supporters, as they claimed to be, who resided in that locality. They held protest meetings and invited me to explain my stand. When addressing the angry citizens, I took the precaution of being accompanied by a member of the City Engineers Department so that questions could be answered if they were of a technical nature. This did not satisfy many people, and I had a good many fists shaken under my nose with the threat that they would 'get me' at the next election. I really did expect to lose quite a few votes over the matter. When the next election rolled around, I received more votes from the very people who resided on the street in question than I had ever had from that area. It taught me an invaluable lesson: people will forgive you for opposing them, but they do not readily forgive fence-sitters.

While in civic politics I learned that one has very little privacy in public life. I had so many interruptions at mealtime that Gordon suggested that we put the telephone right behind my chair at the dining-room table. This arrangement worked very well, and I soon developed other strategies to keep on top of my busy schedule. The *Spectator* carried this story with a cartoon to illustrate it on 15 December 1947: 'Most folks are in bed when they hear the alarm clock go "br-r-r-r." But Ald. Ellen Fairclough, who is also a busy accountant at 2 King Street West, sets her clock in broad daylight to warn her of approaching City Council committee meetings. "I set the clock to go off 15 minutes before a meeting," Ald. Fairclough admitted. "Otherwise, I get busy in the office and don't notice the time pass. Also, it helps impress upon a visitor that I have to be somewhere else soon. It's much more impressive than just saying I have to be at a meeting now." '

I also developed a practice of writing down everything that I had to do, even if it were several months in the future. That way I could organize my time efficiently and not worry about forgetting commitments. When I woke up in the morning I would consult my schedule and get on with what was immediately at hand. Both Gordon and Howard also kept to tight schedules, so at home I was just one of three busy people.

There were also opportunities that went along with my hectic schedule. In June of 1947 I took the train to Vancouver to attend a meeting of the Canadian Wholesale Grocers' Association. Meanwhile, Gordon and Howard drove west to meet me. Howard was equipped with a special 'permissive' licence so he could help with the driving. For a fifteen-year-old boy this was a great adventure. We motored back to Hamilton together, making a detour for yet another IODE conference.

Despite what seemed to be a well-organized approach to life, both my accounting practice and my private life suffered from the demands placed on me by my public commitments. In a glowing *Globe and Mail* article of 28 June 1946, journalist Eva-Lis Wuorio claimed that I handled 'four man-sized jobs with the ease of a trapeze artist on a sky-high tight rope,' but I knew better. As the first member of the Hamilton City Council to be a mother, and a rare woman in the business world, I often found my tight-rope act difficult.

In the summer of 1947, Howard contracted poliomyelitis. Gordon and I were devastated but helpless to do anything except visit him in the horribly inadequate isolation hut at General Hospital. There, we could only talk to him through a screened window. As more and more patients arrived, the pressure on accommodation became critical. Although City Council was being urged to do something about the problem, it appeared unable or unwilling to take it seriously. One day, Dr McIlwraith telephoned to ask if I would accompany him to the hospital, where he took me to an upper floor to look down on the grounds. He then pointed out to me an empty building, which had once been a military hospital but was no longer in use. There it stood, while the polio victims suffered in the crowded isolation building in the intense heat of a Hamilton summer.

I subsequently brought up the subject of the polio ward at a committee meeting of Council. When my comments met with shrugs and general lack of interest, something inside me snapped. Under the stress of emotion, I quietly said: 'Well, you would be more concerned if your son was in that ward, as mine is.' That did it! In no time the patients were moved into the other building, which was well equipped to handle them. Dr McIlwraith was pleased, and so was I.

Howard was in hospital for three months and came out on two canes. Mrs Vanderhar, who was in charge of the ward, had told us that she thought that Howard would never walk again, but she was now pleased with the progress he was making. The day we brought him home, he sat in a big armchair in our living-room and said, 'Did you think I would never walk again?' I fought back the emotion that almost choked me and finally said, 'No, I didn't think that you would never walk again. I thought that you wanted to play the organ again so badly that you would find a way to make those legs work.' And that was exactly the right thing to say. His eyes lit up. He still had a long, hard road ahead, but he worked diligently at his exercises, and Gordon took instruction at the hospital on the manipulation of Howard's legs. Although Howard informed his father that he was not as strong as Mrs Vanderhar, whose wrists were like those of a sculler, the home care seemed to work just as well.

Howard was keen on basketball and had been promised a position on the team at Westdale Collegiate. When he asked the doctor what he could do, he was told that he could do whatever he chose to, but that he must stop if he felt the least strain. Basketball, in particular, was not advised because of the sudden movements and quick stops that were required. Howard was heartbroken.

Participation in sports was a requirement in high school, so Howard was forced to go to the athletic field even if he only sat on the bench. One day he came home from school in a foul mood, his face dark with emotion. I asked what was bothering him, and he said that while he was sitting on the bench the athletics instructor had said to him, 'What is the matter with you, Fairclough? Are you a coward? You can toss the ball around but quit when the going gets tough.' Howard's attitude toward school was never the same after that and I regret that I did not go to the school and 'raise proper hell.' I fear that I had too much respect for the educational system and thought that they were above reprimand. How wrong I was!

Although the playing field was out, Howard was a hero in the auditorium, where his musical talent was much in demand. Sometimes he would be missing from class because he had acceded to the request of another teacher to 'help out with the music.' When he was sixteen, just old enough to join the musicians' union, Kate Aitken, who was in charge of women's affairs at the Canadian National Exhibition (CNE) in Toronto, hired him to play for the fashion parades there. He led the music in several churches in Hamilton and Toronto. After a couple of months at one of his first churches in Hamilton, he was dismissed because people were not going to be dictated to by a young (then seventeen-year-old) 'whipper-snapper.' He went immediately to Royce Presbyterian Church in Toronto, which had a much larger choir and a better organ than the one he had left. Among his other churches in Hamilton were his own church, All Saints, St Luke's Anglican, and James Street Baptist. He was also an accompanist for a term with the Dofasco Male Choir. For more than twenty years he was the organist and associate choir leader, with Lloyd Oakes, for the Scottish Rite in Hamilton.

After he left school, Howard worked as pianist and organist (electric) for Ozzie Williams, band leader at the Club Kingsway in Toronto. When its owner, 'Babe' Kerim, added a second dance floor, he asked Howard to form an orchestra and lead it in the new room. Howard loved this work, and his dedication showed in 1954, when Hurricane Hazel wiped out the road leading to the Kingsway. Undaunted, he walked along the railway tracks that spanned the Humber to get to work. Although music was his first love, Howard also worked with his father at Fairclough Printing Company and he would eventually assume control of the company when Gordon retired in 1980.

Following Howard's illness, I become active in the March of Dimes organization (subsequently renamed the Rehabilitation Foundation). I was a member of the Provincial Board, and in 1956 I was the Chief Marching Mother for Ontario. These women were a hard-working and dedicated group who marched to raise funds for research and facilities, originally for polio victims but ultimately for people with all manner of disabilities. In later years, we were fortunate to incite the interest and cooperation of Philip Rosenblatt, a friend and co-director of Hamilton Trust, who made available two sites for workshops, making the necessary building adjustments to provide easy access for the workers.

During my aldermanic tenure, Gordon took a great deal of 'ribbing' because his wife was in public office. Women were rare in all levels of government, and for many men even one woman in public life was too many. At one gathering in Toronto, someone asked him if he were related to 'the Hamilton Alderman,' to which Gordon replied, 'Yes, she's my wife.' The man then exclaimed, 'She can't be your wife – she must be your mother.' Gordon brought this story home, much to his delight and that of our son, who ribbed me unmercifully.

I eventually got my own back. Later in the same year, I attended a convention of Zonta International in Pasadena, California. It had been a busy and trying few months, and I treated myself to a bedroom on the 'Super Chief' out of Chicago. When I boarded I told the steward that I would like my room made up as soon as possible because I proposed to retire early. He said he would do it as soon as the train cleared the yard and would inform me when my room was ready. Meanwhile, I picked up my 'whodunit' and went to the lounge. I saw no one, since I sat near the door with my back to the rest of the car. In due course, the steward summoned me, and I retired to my room. Shortly, there was a knock on my door. When I answered, the steward handed me a gentleman's business card, on which had been written, 'It looks like a long trip – may I buy you a drink?' I told the steward to thank the man and tell him that I had retired. I then crumpled the card and threw it into the waste-basket. A few minutes later I had second thoughts. I retrieved the card, smoothed it out, and enclosed it in a note to Gordon which said, 'It looks as though someone doesn't think I am your mother.' It was a family joke for a long time.

During this period I had an experience that still haunts me. On 20 October 1949, while I was on my way home from a meeting in Toronto, an elderly man suddenly appeared in front of my moving car, rolled over the hood and fell back again onto the roadway. The accident occurred on Locke Street North, only a few blocks from home. I called for help at a store on the corner. Gordon and Howard came over immediately, and the police were soon on the scene. After the man was taken to the hospital, I was assured that he was not seriously injured. He had no broken bones or internal injuries that they could find. The police concluded that the man was walking from the park to the store when he stumbled on the curb and was just moving to get up when I struck him. This theory was given some credence when the police found the man's handprint on the front bumper. Certainly I did not see him until his head popped up over the front of the car.

I felt that I should attend a memorial service that same evening for Nora Frances Henderson, to be held in the City Council Chambers at eight o'clock, but I was so preoccupied that I could hardly sit still. For a long time after the accident, I had nightmares and my nerves were in a terrible state. Our doctor prescribed medication, which helped, but I shall never forget the horror of that incident.

The sequel of the story did not help matters. The man was in hospital for a few months, during which time they treated him for problems not associated with the accident. According to his nieces, he lived in a room by himself and was in very poor health, in part because he had no teeth and consequently avoided certain foods. They assured me that he had a habit of wandering. In hospital, he actually seemed to improve, but his age and poor health eventually took their toll. The coroner testified that his death could not be attributed to the accident, but I remained troubled. After he died I was subjected to a number of dreadful telephone calls from anonymous people who called me 'murderer' and worse. I suspect the perpetrators were annoyed about some of my political decisions and used this sad occasion to get even.

I was elected to Council in my own right in 1946 and was re-elected for each year through 1949. In late 1949 I ran for the Board of Control and headed the polls, which resulted also in my being appointed deputy mayor.

While I was deputy mayor, Lloyd Jackson got the bright idea that the City should expropriate the Lister Block, directly across from City Hall, so it could be converted into space for civic offices. There was no question that City Hall was cramped, but I thought his solution was ridiculous and did not hesitate to say so. My research included looking at the costs to acquire, renovate, and occupy, the new space, as well as the financial loss to the city in taxes. My remarks were reported in the *Spectator*, which incensed Mayor Jackson. Since I was in the middle of my second bid for a seat in the House of Commons, Jackson thought he could get his revenge by having his friends at the Liberal headquarters in Toronto throw even more resources against me in the campaign. At a meeting of the Board of Control held on the very day that I was quoted in the press, Jackson shook his fist at me and said that he would get me and that I would 'never get elected.' Of course, the reporters immediately departed, and within a short time the incident was 'on the air.' Jackson's behaviour earned me considerable sympathy and support – quite the opposite of what he had intended.

Jackson was a good mayor, and this incident did not destroy the respect we had for each other. When the Lister Block scheme fell through, he concentrated on a new City Hall, which was a much better idea. His driving force was good for Hamilton, and he is commemorated in the naming of Lloyd Jackson Square at the main downtown intersection, King and James.

As deputy mayor, I was frequently asked to stand in for the mayor when he was called away to other duties. One day Jackson asked me if I could attend the Philos Club meeting at noon that day. He neglected to tell me that he was supposed to address the gathering, and so I was caught flat-footed when the chairman rose and called on me to speak. As we were in the midst of budget preparations, there was plenty to talk about and the affair went off very well – I think! This experience helped me get over the fear of giving impromptu speeches, which in my subsequent political career I was often required to do. In politics it is a good idea if public speaking becomes as easy as private conversation; otherwise, one is under a constant strain, anticipating the next call to say 'a word or two' at a function. By the time I had settled into my career in civic politics, I was delivering about fifteen public addresses a year.

The by-election in which I won the seat of Hamilton West in the House of Commons was held in May 1950, halfway through the civic term. Jackson encouraged me to finish out my term by pointing out that the House was about to recess for the summer and that, by the time it was recalled, it would be autumn and only a month from the civic election. He was particularly anxious that I should remain because City Hall was in the thick of a dispute with the 'outside workers' that blew up that summer into a garbage strike.

As the heat soared and garbage piled up, tempers in Hamilton reached the boiling point. Someone threw a large rock at our front door, which made a dent at least a quarter of an inch deep. Fortunately, the door was sturdy, and it withstood the onslaught, but the mark remained. On another occasion, Gordon and his staff were having their office corn roast in our kitchen (they were rained out at Hidden Valley Park) when fire-engines came roaring down our street and stopped outside our house. Angry strikers thought that it would serve me right to be routed out of bed in the wee hours of the morning by a false alarm. Since we were still awake, it probably annoyed the neighbours more than it did us.

In hindsight, I would have had an easier summer had I simply submitted my resignation. Perhaps Jackson got his revenge after all.

PART THREE
The Ottawa Years
1950–1963

ELECTED TO THE HOUSE OF COMMONS in May 1950, at the age of forty-five, Ellen Fairclough was the right woman for the times. The Cold War between the United States and the Soviet Union made conservatism – as long as it was tempered by democratic idealism and humanitarian values – an increasingly popular option. Though the Progressive Conservative Party failed to win many seats under the leadership (1948–56) of former Ontario Premier George Drew, it would attract more support under Prairie populist John Diefenbaker. Both men came to recognize in Fairclough the qualities that had made her popular with the people of Hamilton: honesty, loyalty, and determination. Like her counterparts Margaret Bondfield and Frances Perkins in Britain and the United States, respectively, she also brought a progressive approach to her political career, but one especially tailored to the 1950s.

Ellen worked hard in her new role. Hers was not an easy task. As the only woman in the House during her first Parliament, she was the object of close scrutiny and subject to trivializing comments from colleagues and the press. Many women, unaccustomed to seeing one of their own in such an elevated position, questioned her ability to do the job. In the face of these challenges, she was a 'good sport,' refusing to take offence even when it was offered, and being 'one of the boys,' while at the same time remaining very much a 'lady.' She handled the difficult balancing act with apparent ease, secure in the support of her husband, Gordon, who was a pioneer in his own right as a male political spouse.

In Parliament, Ellen emerged as one of the stars of the opposition benches. Appointed chair of her party's Labour Committee in 1951, she spoke frequently on matters of public interest: unemployment insurance, old age pensions, the post office, and human rights. She gained nation-wide attention with her successive private member's bills to ban discrimination in hiring on the basis of sex, colour, and religion. No friend of the Communists, whose antics she had witnessed at close range in Hamilton, she nevertheless took a strong public stand with unionists opposed to Hal Banks, the American union boss whose goon-squad tactics made a mockery of democratic principles. Criticized at the time for being one of the Conservative Party's Cold Warriors, in later years she would be labelled a 'Red Tory,' a Conservative with a liberal view of social policy.

The first woman to sit in a Canadian cabinet – as Secretary of State (1957–8), Minister of Citizenship and Immigration (1958–62), and Postmaster General (1962–3) – Ellen came to be counted among John Diefenbaker's most resilient ministers. As she explains in this section, she found cabinet life frustrating at times, but she enjoyed the opportunity to effect changes in public policy. She came to office without an agenda but quickly grasped what needed to be done. During her brief tenure as Secretary of State, she initiated Dominion Day celebrations on Parliament Hill. At Citizenship and Immigration, she championed legislation to give Canada's status Indians the vote and introduced reforms in immigration policy to eliminate descrimination on the basis of racial and ethnic origin. She had less success in reorganizing the highly contentious immigration procedures, which were repeatedly thrown into disarray by special pleading, intense media attention, and outright corruption. Ellen and the government she served were defeated at the polls in April 1963, just when Ellen's accounting skills might well have been used to advantage in the Postmaster General's portfolio.

Marginal to the battles within the party in the dying days of the Diefenbaker Government, Ellen had also lost touch with her constituents. Her much-vaunted Loyalist roots meant little to the growing number of Hamiltonians who traced their origins to continental Europe and Asia, while her loyalty to Diefenbaker in the final days of his government was misunderstood by those who had become disenchanted with the 'western maverick.'

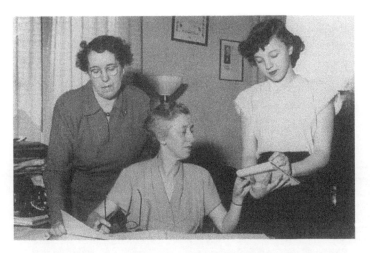

With office staff preparing for the 1949 campaign in Hamilton West. (Photo by Murray Laws)

A 1950 campaign photo with my son and Pat Hopkinson; note the Studebaker! (Photo by Bochsler Studios, Ltd.)

By-election night, 15 May 1950: with Gordon, Mary Heels, Joan Heels, and Pipe Major John MacFarlane

Entering the House of Commons, 30 May 1950, with George Drew and Frank Lennard. (Photo by Capital Press Service)

With George Drew and the House's new loudspeaker system, November 1952. (Photo by Bill and Jean Newton Photography)

George Drew and Gordon Graydon, with Sergeant Dobbin, 7 May 1953. (Photo by Bill and Jean Newton Photography)

Opening of Parliament, 12 November 1953. (Photo by Capital Press Service)

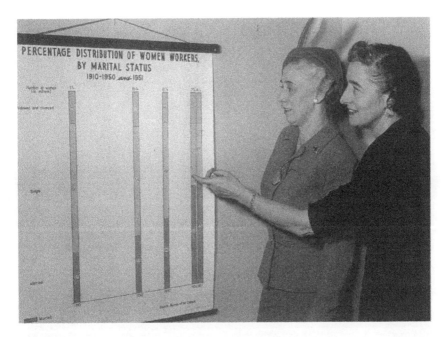

With Alice K. Leopold, Head of the Women's Division, U.S. Department of Labor, Washington, DC, January 1954. (Photo by Ankers)

Grassick cartoon, *Toronto Evening Telegram*, 29 June 1954

Getting instructions from Flight-Lieutenant H.A. McLeod for my flight from Zweibrucken to Marville, August 1955

With Nora Wren (left) and Nellie Howell, founding convention, Canadian Labour Congress, 23 April 1956. (Photo by Fednews)

Marching Mothers, March of Dimes campaign, Hamilton, 1956.
(Photo by Lloyd Bloom)

With two leadership contenders, John Diefenbaker and Donald Fleming, at a pre-convention caucus meeting, October 1956. (Photo by Dominion-Wide; courtesy of Thomson Newspapers)

Equal pay legislation passed, December 1956. (Photo by John Boyd)

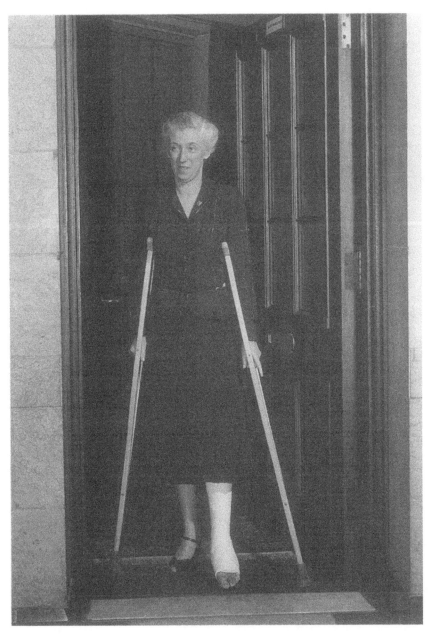

Entering the House on crutches, March 1957. (Photo by Capital Press Service)

Neapolitan Serenade, 6 June 1957. (Photo by J.H. Marsh)

Alf Brooks kidding Don Fleming after swearing-in ceremony, 21 June 1957.
(Photo by Capital Press Service)

Cartoon by Jack Boothe, *Hamilton Spectator*, 25 June 1957

Secretary of State with the Great Seal, 1957

Omar on election night, 31 March 1958. (Photo by *Hamilton Spectator*)

With Prince Aly Khan and Kingsley Brown, Trinidad, April 1958.
(Photo by Canada Pictures Limited)

With Princess Margaret in Hamilton, 2 August 1958

With George Hees at the opening of the Marine Warehouse, 20 August 1958.
(Photo by Phil Aggus)

With Margaret Aitken (left) and Jean Casselman in the Parliamentary Restaurant after Jean's by-election victory, September 1958. (Photo by Capital Press Service)

Being presented, with Gordon, to Governor General Vincent Massey at Government House, 3 June 1959. (Photo by Photo Features Limited)

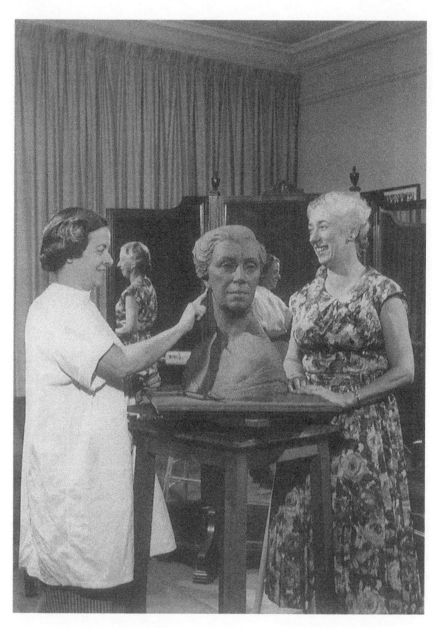
With Betty Holbrook, 11 September 1959. (Photo by National Film Board)

With Deputy Minister George Davidson, 1 May 1960. (Photo by Capital Press
Service)

Visiting with children at a reservation school in Cape Breton, 11 January 1961.
(Photo by Abbass Studio Limited)

Addressing the Annual Meeting, Jewish Immigrant Aid Services of Canada, Windsor Hotel, Montreal, 7 May 1961. Samuel Bronfman is seated to my left.

Lighting the campfire with Dianne Smith, during the Pauline Johnson Pageant, Six Nations Reserve, Brantford, Ontario, 11 August 1961. (Photo by *Hamilton Spectator*)

A light moment with the Prime Minister at a pre-session caucus, 26 September 1962

Daisy and Jim Moodie

'The gang,' from left: June Alston, Diana Urquhart, the author, Jim Moodie, Marguerite Couture, and Willi Gallagher, 8 April 1963

'The last hurrah': Election night, 8 April 1963, with campaign stalwarts
Sud Stephens, Sue McLaughlin, and Neil Kinley

5

Salad Days: The Opposition Years

George Hees (Toronto-Broadview) and I won federal by-elections on the same day, 15 May 1950. Consequently, we were introduced to the House of Commons together on 30 May. It is rather frightening to enter the House after a by-election, for each new member is escorted from the front door to the table of the House. Since I was a woman – the only woman in an all-male House in 1950 – my path had special hurdles. Parliamentary reporter James Roe captured something of the flavour of the day for me when he filed this story, which appeared in the *Ottawa Citizen*:

The ceremony started in an impressive manner. Mrs. Fairclough, dressed in a trim suit decorated with three red carnations, waited in the gloom outside the oaken doors of the House where she was met by Opposition leader George Drew and Frank Lennard (PC-Wentworth).

The two men then escorted her slowly up the floor of the House, and paused at the foot of the House table before the speaker. The only woman member was claiming the right to take her seat – granted affably by Speaker [Ross] Macdonald.

After a moment of confusion, Mrs. Fairclough took her seat, vacated by Mr. Lennard and the House rang with applause. Mr. Lennard gallantly retired to the back bench.

But over the clatter of hands and desks came the raucous tones of Kissing George's [Cruickshank] voice: 'Boy! I could kiss that!' The member for Fraser Valley rushed to the lady's side and planted a decorous but genial kiss on her left cheek.

When Mrs. Fairclough regained her composure, she was welcomed by the Prime Minister who crossed the floor. Then came George Drew and the CCF leader M.J. Coldwell and Labor Minister Humphrey Mitchell, an old Hamiltonian himself.

Mrs. Fairclough will have a single office, the privilege of a lady MP.

In the House she will add a dash of color to the business suits and quiet Conservative ties of her Parliamentary neighbors.

Especially warm will be the new member's welcome by Senator Iva Fallis, who until today had no Progressive Conservative feminine support in the PC caucus this session.

In 1945, Tony Evans had been instrumental in persuading me to run for City Council; he had also encouraged me to run for Board of Control in 1949 after I was defeated in my bid for a seat in the 1949 federal election. When I decided to run again for Hamilton West after Colin Gibson resigned the seat to become a judge, Tony threw his considerable weight behind my candidacy. George Drew, who had become national leader of the Progressive Conservative Party in 1948, after three years as Premier of Ontario, also urged me to run.

After Drew became leader of the national party we had mended our broken fences. Earl Rowe had convinced me that I was foolish to continue to hold a grudge, and I have a strong suspicion that he said the same thing to Drew. Although George was the author of many of his own misfortunes, I now believe he was a much-misunderstood man. What the public took for pomposity was really shyness. He was a highly sensitive man and overreacted to criticism. Because our opponents portrayed him as only a privileged lawyer from Bay Street, it became hard to get him to wear a dinner jacket except at private parties. Drew was a magnificent debater, with a great fund of knowledge. It was a pleasure to listen to him speak. During the years that I served in Opposition, Drew told me things confidentially that he did not tell to any of the other members. He would say to me, 'Now I have told this to no one else,' and he trusted me not to tell even my closest friends. I considered this a mark of great trust of which I was rather proud.

In the 1949 campaign, Drew was careful not take too active a part in preparing the road for my nomination for a federal seat out of fear that local leaders would resent having a candidate shoved down their throats by the 'big boys' in Ottawa. Earl Rowe came to Hamilton for the nomination convention, which was held on 25 May. When my only rival – the Reverend

Norman Rawson, of Centenary United – withdrew from the race, I was unanimously elected to represent the Progressive Conservatives in the riding of Hamilton West. I told my audience that the Progressive Conservative Party was opposed to socialism and the 'dictatorial' methods of the governing Liberal Party and stood for free enterprise, sound government, and policies to provide for the old and children. These were the general themes of the national campaign, and I was careful not to deviate too far from the party line.

George Drew and his wife, Fiorenza, came to Hamilton a week before the election, and both spoke to an enthusiastic crowd of nearly 2,000. During the course of his speech, Drew had some pretty harsh words to say about Communists and was loudly heckled by opponents planted in the audience, but he handled them with ease. Fiorenza was also shouted down when she spoke, making a special pitch to women voters. Fiorenza could really stir an audience and was an even better speaker than her husband. At the 1948 national leadership convention, Fiorenza, who was perfectly bilingual, had given an impressive performance. When she broke into French, our francophone delegates stood on their chairs and threw their hats in the air. She was in her own right a great politician, both in public and behind the scenes.

The incumbent in Hamilton West was Colonel Colin Gibson, a member of the cabinet and a popular politician, who had held the seat since 1940; his father, Sir John, had been MPP for Hamilton and Lieutenant-Governor of Ontario. In encouraging me to run, the big brass in the party were trying to appeal to women voters, the majority of whom seemed to vote for the Liberals. Presumably, they also thought that Hamilton West was a hopeless cause for the Conservatives. They were right. I lost by over 3,000 votes.

Shortly after the election, Colonel Gibson was appointed to the bench, and a by-election was called for 15 May 1950. Many of the riding officers wanted me to make another attempt to capture the seat, and Drew called again, encouraging me to let my name stand. I decided to do so.

Not long before the nomination meeting, I received a call from the riding president, Mr C.R. Drynan. He wanted to see me immediately. A few minutes later he was in my office, with the news that someone was telephoning all the delegates to the nominating meeting asking them to vote for an alternative candidate. The delegate list was supposed to be secret – even I did not know the names. Since the list was left in the capable hands of the President of the Progressive Conservative Women's Association, it was obvious who was to blame. Apparently, some people in the party made up their minds that they did not want a woman candidate. They had secured the services of W. Harry Hopper, a salesman for one of the brewing companies, to make a bid for the nomination. Since he frequented several of the clubs in which working men congregated, he liked to describe himself as 'a friend of labour.'

It did not take long for the news to get around that there would be opposition to my nomination. The Vice-President of the Women's Association endeared herself to me by telling me that she regretted exceedingly what had happened. Although she acknowledged that it was not in her hands to alter the course of events, she and her friends on the executive would do anything in their power to secure my nomination. No doubt the internal opposition to my candidacy encouraged some of the women to work all the harder on my behalf.

I should say at this point that the impetus for my candidacy did not come from the local Progressive Conservative Women's Association. As a working woman I had difficulty attending meetings of the Association, which were usually held in the afternoons. Nor did I have much interest in getting the paid positions, mostly clerical in nature, which were offered to women during the election campaigns. Nevertheless, with the exception of the President, most of the women in our local Association worked hard on my behalf.

The nominating meeting was held in the Crystal Ballroom of the Royal Connaught Hotel in the heart of town. When we arrived at the hall, I found to my delight that my Italian friends were there in full force. A few days earlier, I had attended a meeting of the Marconi Mutual Benefit Society, made up of Italian women whom I had befriended in the course of securing an insurance charter for them. Although they would not be formal delegates, I asked them to attend the nominating meeting as spectators. Their President, Jenny Borsellino, readily accepted the invitation and explained in Italian to those who could not understand that I had extended this invitation to them. On the night in question, they were ensconced in the second and third rows, slightly to the left of the centre aisle, the first row being empty. Mrs Borsellino was a large woman, with reddish grey hair.

She also had an expressive face, which left little doubt how she felt about what was happening around her. Every time anyone mentioned or appeared to support my rival, Mrs Borsellino would lean forward, rest her arms on the back of the chair, and glower at the speaker; when anyone mentioned my name or appeared to support me, she would lean back with a broad, benign smile. Gordon Graydon later told me that her reactions were quite noticeable to those on the platform.

A we had drawn lots, my rival was the first to be nominated. The group supporting him was not, as might be expected, from the ranks of labour but was made up of rather well-to-do citizens. Most of them sat to the left side of the hall, next to and slightly behind my Italian friends. As my rival's nominator approached the platform, Mrs Borsellino leaned forward and favoured him with a most malevolent look. I think it threw him completely, because I have rarely heard a more stumbling speech given in nomination of a candidate. The applause, while polite, was hardly uproarious, and it was obvious that most of it came from the elite group on the left of the speaker. In contrast, my nominator, Argue Martin, KC, made an excellent speech, and Mrs Borsellino beamed at him the whole time he spoke. When it came time for the candidates to speak, Mrs Borsellino and her friends repeated their performance. Although they had no votes, their moral support was inspiring. I had an excellent reception from the audience and a much greater volume of applause than my rival enjoyed.

Gordon Graydon, Member of Parliament for Peel, was the special speaker for the evening. As the returning officers and scrutineers retired to count the ballots, Gordon was called upon to speak. Before he could start, a man from the back of the hall ambled part way up the aisle, obviously suffering no pain whatever. 'Mister Chairman, Mister Chairman, Mister Chairman, who the hell does this man think he is? He calls himself a friend of labour but he has no connection with the labouring man. He's only a beer salesman; Mr Chairman, I object.' Several people rushed towards him in an attempt to evict him, but he managed to fend them off until he had his say. Although the uproar lasted only a few minutes, it was ludicrous in the extreme. Gordon told me afterward that he had had difficulty pulling himself together to start his address. When the votes were counted, they were over three to one in my favour.

It is usually easier to run in a by-election than in a general election. Since the Liberals had won such a large majority in the House in 1949, I could argue that the Opposition needed to be strengthened, which it certainly did. I also scored points on the Liberals' failure to implement universal old-age pensions and to reform the unemployment insurance program. However, I was afraid that I would have little support in the upcoming campaign from the group that had supported my rival. After consultation with George Drew, I secured help from Ottawa, in the persons of Dorothy Downing and Hugh Latimer, from the Ontario Progressive Conservative Party organization. Both were excellent campaigners. In no time they had moved in and superimposed a whole new organizing team over the top of the local one. Eventually, even some of the people who had opposed me at the nominating meeting were beginning to change their tune.

We worked extremely hard. Although the CCF had a strong candidate in Alfred Collingdon and Hamilton was a labour town, the party had little chance of winning the seat. Indeed, a CCF candidate had never won a seat in Hamilton. My real competition was the Liberal, Harold Lazier, a Hamilton lawyer and a son of Judge E.F. Lazier. One of the heart-warming episodes of the campaign was receiving a handwritten letter from his father. Judge Lazier said that he was obviously prohibited from exercising the franchise because of his position on the bench and even had he been able to vote he would have had to cast his ballot for his son; but had the candidate been anyone other than his son he would have been happy and proud to support me. I have kept the letter to this day, and I prize it greatly.

Harold Lazier inherited Colonel Gibson's organization and, despite internal squabbles that racked the Liberal organization in the north end of the city, it ran a vigorous campaign. Nor were its tactics always the most ethical, although dirty political manoeuvres were not new to Hamilton. On the eve of election day, we arrived home around midnight to find that the Liberal organization had been busy covering my signs – including the one on the curb of our own driveway – with signs for its candidate. We immediately phoned Dorothy and Hugh, who got the gang out to undo the damage. What a night that was! They would go around the block only to find that the signs which they had torn down would be back up again. They did not finish until dawn, by which time there were not many signs left for either candidate. Since it was illegal to put up signs after midnight that day – or to tear them down, for that matter – they also had to keep an eye out for the police. At one point a cruiser stopped beside Dorothy, who was in the process of tearing down a sign. She told the officer that he had better look for the people who were out putting up signs on election day, and that retort apparently worked. At least she was not arrested on the spot.

If the campaign was difficult, waiting for the ballots to be counted was worse. The suspense nearly prostrated me, for it was neck and neck the whole evening. Sometimes I would be 100 votes ahead, and then I would slip down, only to come back to 75 above and then back down again. Lazier conceded before nine o'clock, but my margin remained uncomfortably slim. At ten o'clock the final tally was in. I had won by a meagre 406 votes. It was an exhausting night, and one I will never forget. The only consolation was that it must have been even more frustrating for Harold Lazier to lose by such a narrow margin.

The following day, when asked by the *Hamilton News* what I planned to do in the House, I cautiously responded: 'Hamilton West, like the remainder of Hamilton, has an electorate predominantly composed of working people. As the federal member for the riding, I shall do my best to promote and support any and every measure to improve the conditions of the working people.' I went to Ottawa determined to keep an open mind on all issues and to try not to make a disastrous gaff that would destine me to be a 'one-session wonder.'

Between election day and my entry into the House, Eva-Lis Wuorio, a well-known Toronto journalist, followed me around. I had a number of engagements, including an annual meeting of the National Chapter of the IODE in Montreal. From there I went on to Ottawa by train, with Wuorio in tow. At one stage she asked, 'Did you know that the Governor General's car is on the train?' 'No,' I said, being rather innocent in such matters. 'I think I'll send him a note,' she declared. I thought this a little presumptuous, but apparently she had known him for some time. Since it was Viscount Alexander, and he was a most amiable person, I fancy it was not so out of place as I had thought. In any event, we received an invitation to come down to his car for tea. He was a man of easy manner and great wit. During the course of my political career I discovered that most people in high office are quite easy to talk to, and I got used to hobnobbing with people who formerly made me just a little nervous because of their elevated status.

I was the sixth woman to be elected to the Canadian House of Commons. My predecessors were Agnes Macphail (MP 1921–40), Martha Black

(1935–40), Dorise Nielsen (1940–45), Cora Casselman (1945–49), and Gladys Strum (1945–49). In 1949 no women had been elected, and I sat as the only woman from 1950 until 1953, when Margaret Aitken, Sybil Bennett, and Ann Shipley joined me. Female Senators were even thinner on the ground. Cairine Wilson and Iva Fallis, appointed to the Red Chamber in 1930 and 1935, respectively, were alone in a sea of men. Muriel Fergusson, Nancy Hodges, and Mariana Jodoin received Senate seats in 1953.

In my early days in Ottawa I had more support from the men in my party than I did from the women. Many of the women, I think, questioned my ability to do the job, in part because they could not imagine themselves functioning in such a position. Of course, there were a number of professional women who took the larger view of my achievement. The most penetrating media commentary on my election came from Charlotte Whitton, a prominent social worker who, in 1950, was on the verge of a successful career in Ottawa municipal politics. In her column 'Women on the Line' (Timmins *Daily Press*, 31 May 1950), she paid tribute to the women of Hamilton who had laid the groundwork for my victory:

The blot is off the escutcheon for the half-century mark after all, and there will be one woman in the House of Commons as 1950 runs out. She will be as energetic a member as Agnes Macphail, though probably readier to hew the party line than the independent South Grey representative ever would or could be.

Energy and resiliency could well be the characteristic designation of Mrs. Gordon Fairclough, whose surprising triumphant victory over the gallant and popular Colonel Harold Lazier in Hamilton is, at the same time, a tribute to her and to the unusual unity which, for years, has marked the efforts of women in the city of Hamilton. Unless it be Winnipeg, there is no community in the Dominion in which there has been, over the years, such a strong merging of diverse interests among the women to further projects of their common concern, as in Hamilton. ...

Mrs. Fairclough is tall, bright and 'wiry,' we would call her in my part of the country, bright of eye, quick of movement and generally vivacious. She speaks easily, sharply and clearly: she has been forceful and forthright in urging the participation of women in public life and, over a period of years, has consistently practised what she preached on the two home fronts in which we women as a whole have been weak, in which, in fact, most of our representative citizens fail in democracy – in municipal politics and in the ward associations of the parties of our affiliation.

Mrs. Fairclough has come up the hard way, taken on a hopeless looking riding, when put up to fight Colonel the Honourable Colin Gibson last summer. There she made an amazingly good run, but when the Liberals succeeded in getting as candidate Colonel Lazier of the Hamilton Light Infantry, with his brilliant war record, his years of German imprisonment, his warm association with the men and families of his regiment, well the issue was so taken as foregone that Mrs. Fairclough had no serious contender for the convention. The contest was close but her majority adequate. (I myself have lost a wager of a good dinner with Rodney Adamson, M.P., Toronto-York, because I upbraided him for his Party's action in running the capable George Hees in Broadview, which was a 'natural' for Evelyn Macdonald, and Ellen Fairclough in Hamilton, which looked lost.)

The Commons will gain by a woman member again, and a woman in vigorous middle life, both familiar with women's problems and realistically experienced, as controller of one of our greatest industrial cities, in the field of health and welfare, which presents complicated issues in government today.

In the fall of 1950 Charlotte was elected alderman, and, in the following year, she became the mayor of the nation's capital. I had met her in the course of my work with the IODE, and she phoned me from time to time to discuss issues of the day. On one occasion, after she had publicly berated one of her unfortunate subordinates, I suggested that she tone down her flamboyant behaviour. She responded to my advice with a curt 'thank you' and click of the telephone receiver!

Parliamentary life came as quite a shock after the business world. Although I had an office to myself, it was one of the smallest rooms in the Centre Block – a small, pie-shaped affair (No. 544S), squeezed beside the elevator on the fifth floor! There was just enough room for a desk, a sectional book case, a steno's desk, which was jammed up to mine, a sofa (all members had a sofa, I presume for napping, which I never did), a water cooler, and a couple of chairs for visitors. Four persons, in addition to me, made a crowd. Since most male MPs had to share office space with another member, my tiny office at least had the advantage of privacy. When I see the posh suites that even members of the Opposition now enjoy, I realize how much circumstances have changed since 1950. I do not begrudge my successors their good fortune. I think it is only proper that members should have adequate space in which to work and a staff to help them.

My secretary was shared with two Social Credit MPs. (Fortunately I could type.) I also had to pay my own long-distance telephone charges, and many people called me collect, obviously believing that the federal government picked up the tab. While we had a railway pass, it was for coach passage only, and members who travelled any distance had to pay for a berth or room, as well as other expenses en route. There was no air travel pass.

I was greatly amused to find how old-fashioned the whole parliamentary procedure actually was. If I wanted to have a pencil sharpened, my secretary had to go down five floors to use the pencil sharpener in the Secretarial Pool or else sharpen it with a penknife. The supplies available from the stationery office were meagre in the extreme; it did not even have staples, only pins! When it finally began to stock staples, it told members that they would have to supply their own stapling machines. Staplers had been available in most business offices for a couple of decades, but parliamentarians were not to be accorded such luxuries. All this may sound very silly now, but it was one of the aggravations that was particularly acute to someone like me, who had been used to 'normal' office facilities.

Like many other Members of Parliament, I took a room in the Château Laurier, a grand old Canadian railway hotel (where parliamentarians received a special rate) just next to the Parliament Buildings, in the heart of downtown Ottawa. I spent my weekends in Hamilton, taking the train to Ottawa on Sunday night and returning home late on Friday. If there was a special event, Gordon would drive down to Ottawa.

Gordon played the role of the 'spouse' always with good humour and often with enthusiasm. On one occasion, Governor General Vincent Massey was hosting a dinner at Government House and singled us out for his special attention. As he escorted us to the table, he remarked: 'Oh Mrs Fairclough, I am so glad you are here because I want to discuss something with you. I am thinking of having a party for the members' wives.' At this point Gordon interjected, 'Be careful, Sir, that's me you're talking about.' Mr Massey threw back his head and laughed, quite appreciating Gordon's perspective.

When Gordon was not on the scene, I was often chosen to sit next to the host or special guest at a dinner, which meant that I had a chance to talk to a number of fascinating people. Vincent Massey was especially sensitive to my situation and one time approached me in the drawing-room and offered his arm to take me to dinner. His daughter-in-law and official hostess, Mrs Lionel Massey, sat across the table from the Governor General. Massey had a good sense of humour. That evening he admired the gown I was wearing – an ice-blue satin affair, with a bodice of guipure lace, strapless, with a full flowing skirt. 'I dare you to go into the House in that gown later on this evening,' he said. Since the House sat until 11:00 p.m. in those days, it was theoretically possible for me to do so. I made some remark about the difficulties such an appearance would cause, and he said, 'Well, if you will wear that gown into the House, I will put on my false beard and sit in the gallery.' The Governor General, like the Queen, is not permitted to enter the House of Commons when it is in session. In the end, I decided not to accept the challenge.

During my early years in the Opposition ranks I made a number of close friends. Frank Lennard had been a friend before I entered the House and remained one when I got there. As a token of his friendship, he even gave me his seat in the second row of the House so that I would not remain tucked away in the back row, the common fate of new members. Since Earl Rowe was a client of mine, it was natural that we would get together from time to time, usually in the office of Earl's son-in-law, Party Whip Clair Casselman. Art Smith and his wife, Sarah, and Doug and Fran Harkness rounded out our close circle. George Hees and Davie Fulton frequently sought out our company, and George Drew joined us when he could. After the 1953 election Margaret Aitken and Monte (J. Waldo) Monteith were added to our group.

We had some very late nights together, because the House did not rise until eleven o'clock, and many of our gatherings took place after that. The night before the dissolution of Parliament prior to the 1953 election, several of us remained behind to discuss our strategy. It was well past four in the morning when we started walking down the Hill toward the hotel. As we parted from George Drew, someone remarked that it was hardly worth going to bed at all. Drew said, 'Well, it's all right with me if the rest of you want to stay up. I for one need my beauty sleep.' He was a good scout, but it is little wonder that the pressure of the job and the hectic schedule eventually took its toll on his health, and he was forced to resign his position as leader of the party in 1956.

Because I was the only woman in the caucus, I was often called on to speak at nominating meetings. I travelled extensively across the country and made good friends in the process. One occasion stands out particularly in my mind. In May 1951 I spoke at Gordon Churchill's nominating meeting. Gordon had lost his bid for Winnipeg South Centre in 1949 and, like myself, was prepared to give it another shot in a by-election. Although there were some members of the party who felt that Gordon did not have what it took to win the seat, I felt otherwise and told Drew so. Gordon had a distinguished record in two world wars and had been a member of the Manitoba legislature, from which he had resigned to run in the 1949 general election. In addition to noting his obvious support in the riding, I was impressed by the man himself, and I warned Drew to pay no attention to the doubters. I also urged Drew to make sure that adequate financial support was forthcoming. Gordon won that election and continued to hold his seat until 1968, when he retired from active politics. In the meantime he had a successful career both in Opposition and in the Diefenbaker cabinet. I even nominated him for the position of President of the Progressive Conservative Party when George Nowlan stepped down in 1954, but Gordon lost the position to the popular George Hees. Quite apart from his own career, I counted Gordon Churchill as one of my best friends in Ottawa and a tower of strength to me in times of difficulties.

It took me no time at all to learn how difficult it would be to keep out of the limelight that comes with public life. In an address to the Carleton Progressive Conservative Association on 21 June 1950, I criticized the Liberal members of the House for their absenteeism and for 'acting like ten-year-olds.' Such behaviour was the consequence of the big majority on the government side, which meant that many Liberals had little to do. For this comment I was called 'very brash' by the Liberals, who then made much of my failure to vote on two CCF amendments to the Industrial Relations and Disputes Act – because, they alleged, my toeing the Progressive Conservative Party line might offend the labour element in my riding. Actually, I did not vote because I was not involved in the debate and was too busy having my photograph taken!

To balance the bad publicity, I quickly went on record as supporting Old Age Pensions at the age of sixty-five, rather than seventy, which was where the government had decided to peg its Universal Old Age Pension. 'In an industrial city like Hamilton,' I argued, 'it is more than ordinarily important that those who retire from industrial and other work at sixty-five shall be immediately eligible for a retirement pension.' A year later I received a vote of thanks from the Halifax Trades and Labour Council for my consistent stand on issues important to working people, including support for the voluntary, revocable check-off and for taxation of excessive profits.

From the moment I entered the House most media gurus were more interested in my personal life and what I wore than in my political views. I made it clear to anyone who asked that both Gordon and Howard were supportive of my activities and, with the help of a housekeeper, were able to look after themselves. They were, after all, adults. During my campaigns they worked tirelessly on my behalf. Gordon and Howard both did door-to-door canvasses and worked the bars and clubs where a woman's presence was forbidden. Fairclough Printing produced most of my campaign posters and literature. Whenever I needed a pianist to help with campaign rallies, Howard was invariably on hand.

As for my wardrobe, I stuck to business suits and hats for my daily activities, but I chose bright colours (often red or blue) and soft lines to minimize the jarring effect of being the only woman in so many gatherings. Many men became twitchy in the presence of women, so I felt obliged to put them at their ease by looking as feminine as possible. Above all, I wanted to be comfortable. As I told reporter Helen Allen shortly after entering the House, 'You can never do your best work if you don't feel comfortable in your clothes.'

Since the Progressive Conservatives had won only 41 seats in the 1949 election, every member of the caucus was mobilized to keep up the pressure on the government, and Labour soon became my focus. My 'maiden' speech, on 16 June 1950, was essentially a question to the Minister of Public Works concerning the construction of a public building in Hamilton, which it was rumoured would not be built, presumably because the city had voted for an Opposition member. By the beginning of the 1950–1 session I had found my parliamentary voice, speaking long and often.

In 1951 Art Smith resigned his seat for Calgary South because of ill-health. Art had been Chairman of our Caucus Committee on Labour, and George Drew asked me if I would replace him. As Chair of this committee, I became the Opposition spokesperson in the House for all matters related to the Labour portfolio, including the Unemployment Insurance Commission, the Post Office, the Government Compensation Act, and Government Annuities. This was quite a responsibility for a member of less than a year's standing, but I appreciated the trust that George was placing in me and eagerly accepted the challenge.

As Labour critic, I repeatedly criticized the lack of affordable housing in our burgeoning cities, and in June 1951 I began my campaign for a fair employment practices bill that would prohibit discrimination in hiring on the basis of race, colour, sex, nationality, or place of origin. Government Annuities, which many wage earners purchased as a kind of pension plan, also took up a considerable amount of my time.

I did most of the research on the annuity issue myself and I took it quite seriously because it was of interest to urban industrial workers in my riding. When I entered the House, there was a push from leaders in business and insurance circles to allow annuitants to claim cash-surrenders for their investments. The government introduced a bill to implement such a reform. As the debate dragged on, a Special Committee of the House was established to hear the views both pro and con. It was claimed by opponents that some of the annuitants, on receiving the cash, would forthwith abscond with a girlfriend, leaving the wife and family without support. Of course, this comment said more about the speaker than it did about Government Annuities. The upshot of the long and tedious deliberations was that the matter was allowed to die at the end of the session. I like to think that I was in some small way responsible for its demise. Late in the session, I was walking down the corridor with the Chairman of the Committee, who was just as tired of the whole thing as I was. I suggested to him that if he would just let the matter peter out, I would not say a word in the House. To this he agreed, although neither of us knew what might be done by Stanley Knowles, who was leading discussion for the CCF. Fortunately, the bill died.

When the Universal Old Age Pension program came into effect in 1951, Government Annuities were discontinued. However, the problems associated with pensions were equally time-consuming, both for the Minister of Health and Welfare, who at the time was Paul Martin, and me, as Opposition critic. The qualifying age was set at seventy years, and the pension was $40 a month. After the legislation came into effect, it soon became clear that many people reaching their senior years in the 1950s had little idea of their exact age. They had no birth certificates, and baptismal records, if they did exist, had often been lost through fire or negligence. The use of census records also presented a problem, because people sometimes 'altered' the information they gave to the census taker both for themselves and for other members of their family.

Health and Welfare went to great lengths to establish the truth, but it was a time-consuming and often frustrating process. Teams of investigators were sent into hospitals, old age homes, and private residences to interview applicants about their memories of past events so that their approximate age could be established. In a number of cases, people were actually required to send in their family Bibles to document their date of birth. Naturally, many people were loath to do so, fearing loss of this family treasure. As a result of the fears expressed to me by a number of elderly persons, I asked the Minister about the handling and storage of these Bibles – each weighing about twenty pounds – and he assured me that they were being handled with great care and returned promptly to applicants. I must admit that I never heard of any being lost, but the process created considerable unease among those being required to part with their Bibles, and it seemed a very cumbersome procedure when a notarial record might have done just as well.

One of the long-standing concerns of women all across Canada was the double standard in pay scales for men and women. While the government in 1953 sponsored a bill against discrimination in hiring on the basis of race and religion, which covered some of the issues included in my fair employment bill, sex was conspicuously absent. On 2 March 1953, I introduced Private Member's Bill No. 2, calling for equal pay for equal work in areas under federal jurisdiction. Private members' bills are the only way Opposition members like me can get their legislation on the agenda of the House. Such bills rarely pass, because little time is allocated for debate, and in most cases, the governing party is not interested in seeing the credit for a policy go to its opponents. At the end of the session my bill was left on the Order Paper, so I reintroduced it in 1954 and 1955.

When Parliament reconvened in 1956, I was prepared to continue my crusade on the issue, but I was denied the opportunity. As we were waiting the call to the Senate Chamber to hear the Speech from the Throne, George Drew asked me to join him in the front row. 'The Government has paid you a compliment,' he said, and indeed it had. My bill was to be introduced by the Liberals, whose Minister of Labour, Milton Gregg, had finally decided to introduce equal pay legislation. The bill passed, but the Liberals did not get all the credit. In reporting the landmark legislation, the press attributed its achievement to my persistent efforts. The *Globe and Mail* even included photographs of me sitting in front of two piles of money, one representing men's pay and the other, smaller pile, that of women doing the same work. The Château Laurier cooperated in the publicity effort, using its own cash office as a location for the photographs (with the hotel's money, of course).

In the winter of 1953 Gordon's father died, and the Fairclough home at 214 George Street was sold to settle the estate. We were fortunate to find interim accommodation for the summer at 168 Homewood Avenue while our new house at 25 Stanley Avenue was being built. As luck would have it, the federal election was held during this period, which forced us to juggle political and personal matters, to the benefit of neither. Our furniture and many of our possessions were in storage, and we never seemed to be able to find anything that we needed. However, once settled in our new home, we were comfortable. At 25 Stanley, where we still live, we have many of the conveniences that I had long wished for – drawers for long dresses, a storage cupboard for shoes and hats, and a real kitchen.

While serving in Opposition I also took some memorable trips. In September 1952, members of the Commonwealth Parliamentary Association met in Canada. After their deliberations, they set out by private train on a tour of Canada west of Ottawa. Donald Fleming led our delegation to the conference, but he could not take the trip west because of other commitments. When he asked me to take his place on the train, I gladly accepted. We took the CPR route to Vancouver and then returned by the more northern CNR route back through Winnipeg and thence to Montreal for a final banquet. It was quite an experience, highlighted by visits to the capital of each province through which we passed. We were royally entertained along the way. At one station stop, we were treated to a light snowfall, which delighted the delegates, some of whom had never seen snow.

In Saskatoon the delegates were guests at a Chamber of Commerce banquet, at the conclusion of which the Chairman invited them to adjourn to the Saskatoon Club across the street. Since it was a 'stag' club and there were three women in the delegation, this posed some difficulties. The President of Quaker Oats, a friend from my Grocers' Association days, was there that night and came to our rescue. He took us to his suite and eventually to the Ward Room of HMCS *Unicorn*. It was just closing as we arrived but was promptly reopened by the Commanding Officer. In our party were several of the delegates who had left the Saskatoon Club to join us. Among them were a Labour MP from Britain, who insisted on singing although he could not hold a tune; I was charged with the responsibility of accompanying him on the piano. Several others, including Sir Alexander Contanche, bailiff and later governor of the Jersey Islands, soon joined in. Before leaving the club we all sang, 'I don't give a damn for all the rest of Canada – I'm from Saskatoon.' We were having such a good time that we only just made our train, which was scheduled to pull out at 4:00 a.m.! At several subsequent stops one of our happy group, who was much taken with the Saskatoon song, alighted from the train and marched up and down the platform singing, 'I'm from Saskatoon.' Gordon met me in Montreal at the end of our tour and joined us at the banquet, where several members of the Junior League had been recruited to act as hostesses for our primarily male delegation.

We had a lot of fun on the Opposition benches. Before the 1953 election we had a field day over revelations of extravagance and lax accounting practices in the construction of Camp Petawawa. According to the report of investigator George S. Currie, the payroll there had included the names of several horses, and other expenditures failed to stand up to close scrutiny. Minister of National Defence Brooke Claxton had egg all over his face for his failure to control the excesses in his department. It was just the kind of issue that the Progressive Conservatives needed to expose the complacency of the 'Government Party.' George Drew, whose debating skills were unequalled in the House, rose to the occasion most magnificently.

As his birthday drew near, several of us in the caucus decided to honour Drew for his leadership in the Petawawa debate. I played a special role in making arrangements for the ceremony. If I remember correctly, it was Gordon Churchill and Angus MacLean who found a china horse, which they brought to me with instructions to dress it in uniform. This was quite a challenge, but I solved it by procuring some khaki handkerchiefs, which I soaked in water and then plastered on the animal, cutting off the material with scissors and fashioning it into a semblance of a uniform, complete with hat. My colleagues then had it mounted on a base with a plaque which read:

Sergeant Dobbin
Payroll Winner
By Claxton Denial
Out of Currie Report
Trained by Extravagance

An explanatory title read:

Sergeant Dobbin
of the
Petawawa Light Fingered Dragoons
Spur Lifters
Awarded
The Currie Cross
For Incredible
Army Works Services
Far beyond the call of duty

At the birthday dinner, Gordon Graydon, Chairman of the Caucus, presented it to George, and toasts were proposed to him on his birthday and to Sergeant Dobbin for his achievements. Obviously, Opposition members have more scope for their sense of humour than do members of the governing party.

In 1954, as senior female MP, I invited all the women in Parliament to a luncheon in the Parliamentary Restaurant. There were only nine of us: four MPs – Margaret Aitken, Sybil Bennett, Ann Shipley, and I – and five Senators – Cairine Wilson, Iva Fallis, Muriel Fergusson, Nancy Hodges, and Mariana Jodoin. Sybil Bennett and Mariana Jodoin had other commitments, but the rest of us had a great time sharing our experiences as women in the political world.

Following her death in 1954, I was actively involved in having the bust of Agnes Macphail, the first woman Member of Parliament, installed in the Parliament Buildings. On 8 March 1955, the 33rd anniversary of Macphail's introduction to the House, we held an unveiling ceremony just outside the Speaker's chambers, where the bust still stands as a reminder of how recently it is that women received the right to participate in electoral politics.

During this period unemployment insurance was a perennial topic of discussion. I urged the government to eliminate the discrimination against married women that was embodied in the legislation and also demanded that it appoint a woman to the Unemployment Insurance Commission. Since women made up an increasing proportion of the paid labour force (over 20 per cent, according to the 1951 Census), it was only just that their perspective be heard. It was, I believe, because of my insistence that the Department of Labour established a Women's Bureau to focus on issues relating to women in the workforce. I also hounded the government on the level of benefits, supplementary benefits, and delayed payments, which were a constant source of criticism by those who were forced to depend on unemployment insurance. In these matters, I had the hearty support of CCF member Stanley Knowles, on whom I could always count when it came to matters of social policy.

In July 1955 a delegation of parliamentarians was invited to a NATO conference in Paris with a side trip to Canadian military bases in France and West Germany. It was my good fortune to be included. We visited Supreme Headquarters Allied Powers Europe (SHAPE), where we were briefed on SHAPE activities and NATO problems by the 'top brass.' It was a very interesting few days, and valuable for the first-hand information provided on the activities of SHAPE and NATO at the height of the Cold War.

All was not work, though. We took a boat tour of the Seine, from which we viewed Notre Dame and other sights of the romantic city. Despite the exceptionally warm weather, we enjoyed the receptions hosted by French officials and visits to Versailles, the Luxembourg Palace, and the Eiffel Tower. It was at Versailles that I saw my first 'light and sound show,' at which the delegations were guests. One almost felt the presence of the historical characters portrayed.

On one day when there was no official function, I decided to explore the Metro, which was impressively clean and efficient. I consulted maps of the system, selected destinations, and went to the surface at each to have a look around before descending to travel again. The rest of the day was spent touring the Louvre and Montmartre – what a view!

While visiting our bases, Squadron Leader William Lee, who was also from Hamilton, gave me the opportunity to sample jet flight. I had been lamenting the fact that I had not flown in a jet, and he arranged for Senator

Muriel Fergusson, Paul Hellyer, and me to take a spin in a T33 bomber (one assigned to each of us). Before boarding, we were given detailed instructions on how to manipulate the ejection seat, issued flight suits, and strapped into parachute harnesses which were so heavy that I could barely climb into my seat. Once installed, I was again instructed as to the use of instruments that I might (possibly) be called on to use. We took off for Marville with great fanfare and were escorted by other craft, subsequently landing, without any problem, at our destination.

As I scrambled out of my aircraft (*sans* parachute, from which I was released on landing), Squadron Leader Lee greeted me with a broad smile and asked me how I enjoyed my flight. I said I was greatly disappointed because I had expected a sensation of speed; instead, we just seemed to dawdle along. Moreover, the noise was greater than that of a boiler factory. It turned out that we had, indeed, flown at a slow speed and at only about 5,000 feet. The height at which the parachutes were operable was 15,000 feet! Then I knew that we had been 'had' and could understand the look of amusement on the faces of the crews and staff. They presented us with matchbooks, with our photos on the covers, as souvenirs.

In June 1956 the Minister of Health and Welfare, Paul Martin, introduced a bill that represented a major overhaul of the unemployment insurance legislation. There were extended discussions both in Committee and in the House. As Chairman of the Caucus Committee on Labour, I was responsible for marshalling our party's forces to debate this complicated and far-reaching legislation. Research facilities were practically non-existent for Opposition members. The most we could hope for was a pile of books from the Parliamentary Library, produced by a member of the staff of the Leader of the Opposition, with slips of paper inserted at the appropriate page to be investigated.

Faced with a deadline and daunting responsibilities, I solved my problem by hiring a retired official of the Unemployment Insurance Commission to do some research for me. He did an excellent, clause-by-clause comparison of the old act and the proposed changes in the new act. I organized this information into a loose-leaf ring-binder, with the old and new clauses on facing pages. My 'retired official' also gave me useful advice on the likely effects of the new proposals, and his informed opinion was invaluable in the ensuing discussions, both in Committee and in the House. I (gladly) paid for his services out of my own pocket. The research assistance that is available to Members of Parliament today is to be envied.

As it turned out, we had less opportunity to debate the bill than I would have liked. If my memory serves me well, the bill was made available to members at noon one day in June and was to be introduced and debated that same day. The Caucus Committee on Health and Welfare was chaired by Dr William Blair, but he asked me to lead the debate for the Opposition, because, as he said, 'You know more about this than I do.' I could sympathize with him, and the subject really had more to do with Labour than with Welfare, so I acquiesced. He made this request as I was leaving the afternoon session of the House, barely two hours before the debate was scheduled to commence.

I had little time to pull my thoughts together. I had no dinner that evening. At eight o'clock, when the House resumed sitting, the Minister came over to my desk and said that he had a favour to ask me. He explained that his Deputy Minister, George Davidson, was due to sail at midnight to attend a conference in Europe and could not leave until the bill had been passed in the House. Apparently, Dr Davidson's wife was already on board the ship. He asked me if I would consent to make my remarks as brief as possible, consistent with a full examination of the bill's contents. It seemed like a reasonable request, and, accordingly, I agreed.

I assume that he approached other Opposition parties also, because the bill reached the Committee stage in good time, but not before the Minister managed to 'sum up' his presentation with a particularly partisan speech on the virtues of the government, declaring that no other party would bring in such enlightened legislation. 'These measures,' he concluded, 'round out to a very complete degree a measure of responsible social welfare action in this country of which all Canadians can be proud. ... it is the only group that will ever be in power to do these very things.'

I was furious, knowing full well that he had taken advantage of my willingness to cooperate. I rose in the House to remind him of the fact and warned him: 'if the Minister wants to get his bill through the House, he jolly well had better quit making political speeches.' I went on to say, 'After obtaining the cooperation of this House, the Minister believed that he could cram this down our throats in a very short space of time. ... I would not have spoken in this vein, Mr Chairman, had it not been for the smart-alec interjection of the minister at the last minute. I think his attitude in that respect leaves much to be desired.' The only bright spot was that Dr Davidson was able to make the ship on time, and a few years later, when he became my Deputy Minister in the Department of Citizenship and Immigration, he could not hold against me the fact that I had delayed his trip to Europe.

As the Opposition critic for Labour, I certainly had my hands full. George Drew and I worked closely on issues related to Labour, but I was the one who had to stand up in the House and get the party's position across. The Hal Banks affair was my baptism of fire. Banks was a ruthless union leader who was invited to Canada in 1949 by shipping interests, in collusion with government and certain segments of organized labour, to destroy the Communist-controlled Canadian Seamen's Union (CSH). His attempts to expand the jurisdiction of the Seamen's International Union (SIU), over which he presided, precipitated bloody conflict in Canadian seaports. I am convinced that Labour Minister Milton Gregg was embarrassed by having to defend Banks, but for reasons that are still not clear to me he continued to support him both in and outside the House. In 1954 I vigorously opposed the nomination of Hal Banks to represent Canada in the International Labour Organization, not only because of his unsavoury record but also because he was not a Canadian. George Drew and I were frustrated in our attempts to have Banks replaced, one of the reasons being the unavailability to us of American criminal records.

What I had not bargained for was being intimidated myself. At the height of the debate in the House, I received several telephone calls warning me to 'lay off or else.' I appreciated the serious nature of the threats but doubted that any harm would come to me, because any overt action would only confirm rumours of the strong-arm tactics that supposedly characterized Banks's style. One day two CSU members called on me to verify the 'goon' tactics of Banks's enforcers; they both bore the scars of brutal beatings, and I was shocked. In addition to the personal calls I received, numerous letters came outlining the tactics employed by Banks, but unfortunately this information could not easily be substantiated.

A sad consequence of the Banks affair was the resignation of my secretary. A quiet, middle-aged woman of somewhat timid character, she was convinced that both she and I were in great peril. It affected her to the point where she had hallucinations that thugs were climbing into her third-storey apartment to get her. She had to leave her job and take treatment in a psychiatric hospital. Although she eventually recovered, Banks and his hench-men left an indelible imprint on her mind.

Banks was finally convicted in 1964 for the merciless beating of Henry Walsh. Sent to Montreal's Bordeaux jail, he was released after two weeks on $25,000 bail and promptly disappeared. The full story of Banks and his activities is a fascinating record of deceit, murder, larceny, and, I'm sorry to say, collusion by many in industry and government, who must surely have ultimately hung their heads in shame. He certainly was the nastiest 'piece of goods' that it was ever my misfortune to encounter.

I was privileged to have many supporters and good friends among the ranks of labour in Hamilton. Although they may not have been of my polit-ical stripe, their advice and support (sometimes surreptitious) was invalu-able in a constituency with a large proportion of wage labourers, many of whom were unionized. Gordon was particularly adept at maintaining close ties with union men and advised me on issues that mattered to them. When I became Secretary of State, I went on record as supporting the use of unionized shops for printing contracts and tried to keep in touch with the labour position on major issues.

I was invited to attend the First Constitutional Convention of the Cana-dian Labour Congress (CLC) in April 1956. The merging of the Canadian Congress of Labour and the Trades and Labour Congress of Canada to form the CLC marked a milestone in labour organization in Canada and reflected a similar merging of the American Federation of Labour (AFL) and the Committee for Industrial Organization (CIO) in the United States. In attendance from Hamilton were, among many others, two women from the textile industry, Nora Wren and Nellie Howell, with whom I was pho-tographed. The same courtesy was extended to me by the two heads of their respective Unions, Aaron Mosher (CCL) and Claude Jodoin (TLC). My memorabilia include the badge that was issued to me as a 'registered Guest.' Unfortunately for the Progressive Conservatives, the CLC threw its weight behind the New Democratic Party when it was created in 1961.

As Labour critic, I spoke frequently on matters pertaining to the Post Office. Little did I know that some day I would be in charge of that diffi-cult department. One of the matters that caused real concern in my own riding was that postal carriers were deemed to be earning too little to qual-ify for the purchase of a home under the proposed National Housing Act in 1953. I drew this matter to the attention of the Minister of Public

Works, Robert Winters. The government, I pointed out, paid the salaries of these men and also set the rules under which they could qualify for a mortgage.

During my perusal of the Post Office Estimates in 1954 I noticed an item called 'Uniforms and Mail Bags.' The local postal carriers in the Hamilton area had told me that although they were measured for their uniforms, the outfits did not fit 'worth a darn.' When the item came up for consideration, I asked the Postmaster General if the uniforms and mail satchels were made by the same supplier, because my informants said that 'the mail bags fit better.' There was a lot of laughter in the House, which was not appreciated by the Minister. Subsequently, there was a cartoon by Grassick in the Toronto *Telegram* depicting me as a designer of uniforms. The original hangs on my wall, courtesy of Mr. Grassick.

The closing weeks of the 1956 session were stormy ones. Minister of Trade and Commerce C.D. Howe tried to ram the Trans-Canada Pipeline bill through the House by invoking closure, and we fought the government tooth and nail. At one point in the debate, Don Fleming was ejected from the House by the Speaker. I anticipated this dramatic moment and, after getting Drew's approval, sent word to my secretary to find a Red Ensign. As Don left the chamber I draped his empty seat with the flag that I had managed to secure about twenty minutes before the Speaker issued his dictum. I received a lot of publicity for this symbolic act. Although I was criticized by some people for showing disrespect for the Canadian flag, it dramatically made the point that the rights of free speech were being muzzled by a dictatorial government. This would be a familiar refrain in our party as we geared up for an election which was expected in 1957.

Before the election was called, George Drew resigned. The pipeline debate had taken its toll on his health, and his doctor told him that he must reduce his commitments or face an early death. I was among the selected few, which included Fiorenza, Earl Rowe and his son Bill, Grattan O'Leary, editor of the *Ottawa Journal*, and Jim Macdonnell, Member of Parliament for Toronto-Greenwood, who met in a room at the Royal York Hotel in Toronto to discuss George's fate. He really had no choice. Since I could type, I volunteered to go with Bill Rowe to the Albany Club to type Drew's letter of resignation, which had been drafted by Grattan O'Leary. I made a copy for my scrapbook, which was signed by most of the people in the room. It was a sad day for all of us, but especially for Fiorenza, who was more aware than any of us of the bad state of George's health.

Shortly thereafter, we were deeply involved in a leadership convention. John Diefenbaker emerged as leader of the Progressive Conservative Party, and within six months we were facing a general election, set for 10 June 1957. I had won the 1953 election by a majority of nearly 3,000 votes and was quite confident that I would do well again. How the public would respond to our party under Diefenbaker's leadership was anybody's guess. Before Drew's resignation, there were a lot of people, not all of them supporters of the Progressive Conservative Party, who maintained that Diefenbaker was the man of the hour. He had refused to cooperate with Drew, to the point of refusing to attend committee meetings, but he cultivated the press and had won widespread support for his willingness as a lawyer to champion the underdog in court. In all likelihood, Diefenbaker made the difference between victory and defeat for our party in 1957, but his leadership style bothered many people in the party that was now responsible for running the country.

6

Endless Days: The Cabinet Years

With an election looming, my sister Mary came to Ottawa for a weekend in February 1957 to help me plan promotion and organization. On Saturday the 23rd, we went to Hope's book shop on Sparks Street for supplies. On leaving, I tripped and fell on the tile floor, my head just missing the heating radiator. The pain in my lower left leg was excruciating. With Mary's help I managed to crawl back into the store, but I could put no weight on my left foot. We returned in a taxi to the Parliament Buildings, where I went directly to the masseur who had an establishment in the basement. I had visited him many times for steambath massage. As a former manager of the Ottawa Roughriders, he knew exactly what to do. He told me that I had torn ligaments in my foot and leg, and he proceeded to tape them up securely. Even with the taping and the aid of Mary's strong arm, I had difficulty getting back to the hotel. Once I was there, the staff made a wheelchair available for the long corridor that I had to negotiate to my room.

I called George Drew for advice, and he referred me to his physician, Dr Whitely, who asked me to come to his office in the hospital. Once more the wheelchair routine. Dr Whitely's examination confirmed the masseur's findings. Since he could not improve on the bandaging, he suggested I wait until the swelling went down, at which point he would put the leg in a cast. In the meantime, I was to stay in bed and rest. My visions of a door-to-door campaign in the near future were receding fast! A couple of weeks later I was in a cast and hobbling around on crutches.

It was several weeks before the cast was removed, by which time we were in the midst of the campaign. The first thing I did was start visiting door to door in Hamilton West, much to Gordon's concern. A new survey had been opened in the extreme southwest of my riding, and the roads there were covered in stone in preparation for paving. It was in this area that I intended to do my first 'blitz.' My workers went down each side of the street, and when householders appeared they hailed me and I would hurry across the loose stone to greet them. This procedure went on for a couple of hours, with Gordon following in his car. I was very careful because I did not want to take another tumble, which could have resulted in even greater damage to my poor leg. Although I managed to make it back and forth across the rocky road, at the end of the day I subsided onto the seat of the car, my leg aching like a bad tooth. Would I be able to continue down the campaign trail? When I got home I sat at the edge of the bath tub and let the water run, first cold, then hot, for about a half an hour. The treatment seemed to work, but when I told Dr Whitely about my rocky exploits and the subsequent treatment he was aghast. He said that, if consulted, he would have advised me to rest, with my leg elevated on a stool or chair.

Despite my handicap, I did well at the polls on 10 June, taking more votes (16,533) than my two opponents, John Munro (Liberal, 9,964) and William Scandlan (CCF, 4,363) combined. We Conservatives were all pleased to be in a position to form the government, but our minority status (112 of 265 seats) made it certain that we would be facing another election within a short time.

We were sworn into office on 21 June 1957. As we were leaving the Governor General's residence, with our heads swelled by the importance of it all, someone asked Don Fleming if his hat still fitted his head. A photographer snapped a picture of me pointing at Don's hat, just as I was explaining to George Hees what everyone was laughing at. It turned out to be one of the most candid photos of the Diefenbaker cabinet and was widely published in the press.

When I became a cabinet minister I quickly realized that I had powers unavailable to the ordinary citizen. My reputation in Hamilton soared when, in the summer of 1957, I intervened to assist the Hamilton Tiger-Cats football team. On returning from Ottawa one Saturday morning, Gordon met me at the station with the message that Jake Gaudaur and Ralph Sazio were waiting at our home to see me. They wanted to enrol a California-based football player, but their roster of imports was full. This man apparently had a Canadian father and could claim Canadian citizenship but had to do so by the age of twenty-two. Since the young man was below the age limit and was prepared to take out citizenship, there was no problem, except that the deadline for registering with the Canadian Football League was only two days away. Of course, it was Saturday and no federal offices would be opened until Monday, so the chances of meeting the deadline were slim.

I immediately phoned Davie Fulton, who was acting Minister of Citizenship and Immigration, and he promised to see what could be done. He had Gaudaur and Sazio come to Ottawa with the necessary papers. Everything was accomplished with astonishing efficiency. And so it was that Gerry McDougall became a Tiger-Cat. I am told that he still holds the Canadian record, as a running back, for the most carries, 805, most yards, 4,270, and the most touchdowns, 29. (I am indebted to Ralph Sazio for the statistics.) The story eventually got out that I had been involved in the efforts to establish Gerry's citizenship, and I was delighted to accept the blame – or the credit.

Other goals took longer to achieve. The centre pier supporting the swing railway bridge in the ship canal leading from Lake Ontario to Hamilton Harbour had long been a navigational problem for freighters using this waterway. As the ships grew in size following the Second World War, the problem became even greater. While in Opposition I had made a habit of scanning the Estimates of Public Works to see if any action was proposed, but I searched in vain. When the government changed in 1957, I continued to badger the Minister of Public Works (now one of my colleagues) and was told that the resistance was coming from Treasury.

The opportunity to apply pressure presented itself when I accompanied the Prime Minister on a trip to Hamilton. As our plane approached the city, I asked the pilot to fly over the canal. Then I pointed out to John Diefenbaker the difficulties for navigation created by the narrow channels divided by the central pier. The solution was removal of the pier and substitution of a bridge to carry rail traffic. He agreed that the hazard should be eliminated and promised to look after it. I do not know whether the project had already been put on the Public Works list, but the pressure from the Prime Minister certainly helped to speed the project along.

Congratulations poured in from all over the country on my appointment as the first female cabinet minister. I tried to answer all the correspondence and succeeded in dictating a vast number of letters, but, despite the lapse of time, no transcriptions arrived on my desk. One day, Theresa Maloney, the Administrative Assistant to the Deputy Minister, came into my office and said, 'I suppose you are wondering where your dictation is?' I acknowledged that the thought might have crossed my mind. She explained that the stenographers were used to French dictation, so they were transcribing my dictation into French and then translating it back into English, all of which, of course, took time. To my consternation, I found no English-language stenographer in the Minister's office. Although all members of staff were officially bilingual, they had been hired by my francophone predecessor and thought in French, a situation that made for awkward misunderstandings. Fortunately, two of my former secretaries while I had been in Opposition agreed to join my office staff. One of them, Anne Shaw, was employed as a librarian with the Bank of Canada but preferred to work for me. The other, Kate Henderson, had gone to the Embassy of the Union of South Africa, but she happily transferred to my office.

Meanwhile, I called my niece Joan Heels, who was studying music in Montreal and working for Office Overload to make ends meet. She agreed to help me for a couple of weeks until I got my office organized. Firm instructions were issued that she was working personally for me and being paid by me. I did not want it said that the first thing I did as minister was to employ a member of my own family. Joan went through the correspondence like 'a hot knife through butter,' much to the chagrin of the staff, but to the amusement of Theresa. When we were caught up, Joan returned to Montreal. By this time, Anne and Kate had joined my staff and the office was running along smoothly.

As my executive assistant I chose James Moodie, who, with his wife Daisy, moved from Hamilton to help me get settled in my new job. During my years in the cabinet, they allowed me to use their apartment in Ottawa for entertaining and generally gave me a home away from home. Jim came from a prominent Hamilton family, which had owned a knitting goods company. After serving in the Second World War in the 4th Canadian Armoured Division, he worked with General Motors and Minnesota Mining and Manufacturing. He brought considerable experience to my political organization in Hamilton, and I was lucky to get him as my executive assistant. Daisy worked as executive assistant for Sam Ross, General Manager of the Ottawa News Bureau, as well as helping me. We were all very busy, day and night, and now wonder where we found our energy.

Jim supervised the acquisition of people for my personal staff and their coordination with the civil servants who worked in my office. He recruited June Alston, Gloria Armstrong, Wilhelmina (Willi) Gallagher, and Diana Urquhart from Hamilton to work with me. Willi became my personal secretary, while Anne Shaw served as my principal secretary in departmental matters. Gloria moved into Indian Affairs. We were a tight-knit group and managed to weather the many challenges that ministerial life entailed.

As a new cabinet minister in 1957, I consulted with our Whip and House of Commons staff concerning where my office would be located. I was given a list of vacant offices of former ministers. Presumably, other ministers were going through the same exercise. I decided that one of the offices on the north corridor would suit me. It had an ensuite washroom and was large enough to house my files and personal effects. Before leaving for a much-needed holiday, I arranged for the move to take place in my absence. When I returned I found my 'office' had been moved into the hall and that some of my valued possessions were missing. Another minister had simply moved in while I was away. Perhaps it would be more correct to say that my new office was occupied by the staff of the Minister, because I do not believe he had anything to do with my ouster. He probably was on holiday, too.

By this time, of course, most of the offices had been taken, and the only available space consisted of part of Louis St Laurent's rooms on the main floor. The accommodation left much to be desired, but I was in no position to object. I moved in and made the best of a poor bargain. When I became Minister of Citizenship and Immigration after the 1958 election, the situation was aggravated by more staff crammed into my inadequate quarters. But I had learned my lesson. Sidney Smith, Secretary of State for External Affairs, died suddenly in 1958. Although we were all aggrieved, we moved quickly to improve my office space. Sidney's Parliamentary Assistant, Wallace Nesbitt, MP for Oxford, had selected a suite on the ground floor near the private entrance to the House. They were elegantly furnished and suited my purposes perfectly. Within an hour of hearing the news of Sidney's death, my staff had moved me into the more spacious offices he had occupied, even to the point of removing the name plates from the former premises and installing them on the new ones. If anyone remarked on the matter or made any objection to the move, I did not hear about it. Sidney would have been amused, I am sure, by the promptness with which we took advantage of the situation.

Sidney's death brought other changes to my department. When a Minister leaves the government for whatever reason, his personal staff is immediately dismissed. Jim Moodie was concerned about Henry Best, who had been Sidney's executive assistant. Since there was a vacancy on our staff, we agreed to hire Henry, who actually helped to relocate my offices. Henry was the son of Charles Best, co-discoverer, with Frederick Banting, of insulin.

Kingsley Brown also joined my personal staff as a Special Assistant. A Nova Scotian by birth, he was working at the *Hamilton Spectator* when we spirited him away to Ottawa. He had the great ability of being able to write speeches that were so close to my own style that I felt I had written them myself. Although officials in the department were responsible for producing speeches of an official nature, particularly with respect to legislation and the administration thereof, I was also frequently called on to speak at functions where my talk would be on a topic not related to departmental affairs. Kingsley conferred with me as to the proposed subject and the points I wished to make. He then produced a draft, which we would go over together. Inevitably I would say, 'Oh, that reminds me,' and then insert some opinion or incident. When finished, the text was so similar to my own writing that it 'felt like me.' Kingsley and I were so compatible that I regretted deeply his decision, a couple of years later, to take an administrative position at St Francis Xavier University. However, he was anxious to return home to Nova Scotia, and he knew that my tenure in office was, at best, precarious.

Kingsley had a deliciously droll wit. One comment he made has remained with me. The Civil Service, he opined, was composed of two kinds of people: those with little or no ability but tremendous ambition, and those with great ability and no ambition. The tension between a Minister's personal and Civil Service staff is never far below the surface and was especially acute during our government. Most of the civil servants had been hired and trained under a Liberal ministry and resented having to adjust to a new regime. I never did hire my full quota of personal staff, which meant that I continued to rely on civil servants, who, for the duration, were transferred to my personal service. However, the difference between personal staff and civil service could never be overlooked.

It is important for a member of cabinet to have someone on staff who has knowledge of the minister's constituency. MPs now usually have constituency offices, but such 'extravagances' were frowned upon by John Diefenbaker. He felt that because he did not need one nobody else did. At the risk of incurring his disapproval, I set up an office with a secretary in the Federal Government Building in Hamilton and hired Laura Arnold, a former employee in my accountantcy firm, to run it. Of course, many Ministers could use their local offices as a base for constituency business, but people like me who had to give up their professional practices on entering the cabinet had little alternative but to establish a stand-alone operation. I heartily agree with the establishment of constituency offices, at both the federal and the provincial levels. It is much easier for the member to keep in touch with the constituency and certainly more convenient for the voters to approach their member.

On the home front, we continued to employ a housekeeper. Two exceptional individuals remained so close to us that we consider them family. In the 1950s Margarete (Gretl) Ranzmeir came to us from Austria. She was young – scarcely twenty years old – but she was an excellent housekeeper and, in addition, had studied dress design, which resulted in some beautiful clothes for me. She had no family ties, and when she married Paul Bass, Gordon 'gave her away' at the wedding, which took place at our home. Paul's father had appealed to me, as Minister of Citizenship and Immigration, for assistance in bringing his family to Canada from Germany. Paul and Gretl's second son, Ronald, is my godchild. Although I was named as the godparent of their first son, Ernst, the minister at the Lutheran Church would not sanction the sponsorship at the christening – probably because I was not Lutheran – but I consider him as our godson also. Gretl and Paul eventually settled in New Zealand, where she became very successful in her own dress design business, which she subsequently sold to a large manufacturer at a substantial profit. Paul also did well in the construction industry.

As Minister of Citizenship and Immigration I was in a unique position to find domestic help. When I needed a replacement for Gretl I simply alerted officials in my department. In short order, they telephoned me from Montreal with the news that a recent arrival in Canada, Rosa Mueller, seemed to have the right qualifications. When she arrived in Ottawa, the interview was difficult for Rosa spoke practically no English; I called in one of my staff to speak to her in French, but unfortunately her French was also limited. Eventually, I had the bright idea of telephoning Gretl in Hamilton, and the two of them chatted away in German, and we finally hired Rosa. It was agreed that if and when she was at a loss for information she would telephone Gretl, who would explain everything, from where the utensils were kept to the kind of food we liked. Within two weeks Rosa was speaking quite acceptable English. Her capacity for language was really quite amazing. She also spoke Italian with the man who delivered vegetables to us and conversed with our son, Howard, in 'high school' French.

Rosa was amazing in other ways as well. She was an exquisite cook, having graduated from the Wirtefachschule restaurant school in Berne, Switzerland. She was also what we used to call 'a real worker.' We had been in the habit of having a 'cleaning woman' come in weekly to do the heavier work, but after a couple of weeks Rosa said that she preferred to do all the cleaning herself. She left our employ after three years when she married Kurt Anderegg. It was a great compliment to me when she subsequently asked me for my recipe for pineapple upsidedown cake. Rosa and her husband now live in LaHabra, California. In June 1988 they visited us with their son and daughter.

When Rosa left we were fortunate to secure a daily housekeeper, Edna Ball, who lived on Upper Garth Street. Edna, too, became part of our family. She came to us for several years until an arthritic condition made it impossible. However, we kept in touch, and on several occasions she 'house sat' for us when we were on vacation.

It is not surprising that once I was sworn into office the press was eager to interview the first woman to become a cabinet minister in Canada. The local TV station, CHCH, recorded my homecoming, with the 'whole' family on hand. The cameraman suggested that I come through the French doors before being seated on the patio, where I would converse with the family. Gordon, waiting patiently as usual, was holding a newspaper. As soon as I was seated, our black retriever, Omar, walked over to him, took the paper from his hands, and presented it to me. Talk about 'scene stealers'! The cameraman was delighted. When over the next few evenings Gordon took Omar for a walk, several people stopped him on the street to ask, 'Is that the dog that was on television?' Omar also stole the show on election night in 1958, when he carried a banner inscribed 'Fairclough Again.'

A Member of Parliament receives a great many letters from the public.

During my time in office it was common to receive requests for an autograph, a photograph, or both. Several times teachers suggested to their classes that they should write to an MP (not necessarily their own) for an autographed photo. Since I was the only woman in Parliament from 1950 to 1953 and the only woman in the cabinet from 1957 to 1963, I received more than my share of these requests. Once I was asked for an autographed picture from forty-eight pupils in one class – poor teacher! – in Saskatchewan. When I became a Minister I did not have to worry about the cost of the photographs, but I had to pay for them myself when I was just a lowly Opposition MP.

As a cabinet minister, I received an enormous number of invitations to speak to organizations both in Canada and in the United States. I accepted as many as I could and instructed Anne Shaw to include in my letter of acceptance the request that there be 'no corsage.' One time the message was interpreted to mean that I was allergic to them, but that was not the case. My reason for not wearing flowers was that the pins in the corsage ultimately made a wreck of my dress. Moreover, it often covered what was the main decoration, usually a piece of good jewellery used to complement the gown. Like many seasoned travellers I sometimes arrived at my destination to find that my luggage had gone astray. I was particularly inconvenienced when I was forced to deliver a speech to the Zonta Club of Memphis still wearing my travelling suit. This time I did wear a corsage, to dress it up a bit, but by the end of the evening I had discarded the jacket of a fairly heavy and entirely inappropriate suit.

Even when we were not in an election year, I travelled extensively within the country. My department records show that I travelled over 50,000 miles on government business in 1959 and never went outside Canada (except for a holiday). In total, I clocked at least a quarter of a million miles in my cabinet career, most of it in Canada. Virtually all of the travel was by rail, since we used air only in emergencies, during election campaigns, and for foreign visits.

My new status resulted in several delightful trips abroad. Following the 1958 election I was one of the government's representatives at the celebrations inaugurating the Federation of the British West Indies. Our delegation then went on to Argentina for the ceremony inducting the new President, Arturo Frondizi. As the only woman representing a foreign country, I received a lot of media attention. Also in 1958 I visited our immigration offices in Great Britain. Gordon went along with me on these diplomatic excursions, making them much more pleasant for me.

Since Margaret Aitken and I were the only women elected in 1957 we could have held a meeting in a phone booth. Jean Casselman joined us when she won the by-election for Grenville-Dundas in September 1958. As the daughter of Earl Rowe and the widow of Clair Casselman, Jean was wise to the ways of political life. The Liberals finally elected a woman to the House when Judy LaMarsh won a by-election in Niagara Falls in 1960. Like Charlotte Whitton, Judy had a rather aggressive style that often got her into trouble. She was the Liberal critic for Indian Affairs and occasionally challenged me in the House, which of course amused the boys in the press gallery, who liked to play up any scrap between two women.

When I was sworn in as Secretary of State in June 1957, I had no idea of the department's scope and was quite surprised at the range of my responsibilities. War Claims, Patents and Copyrights, the Civil Service Commission, the Companies' Act, and the Queen's Printer, among other things, fell under my jurisdiction. As Minister of a 'catch-all' department, I had my work cut out for me. Pressure for a distinctive Canadian flag was also building up, and my department was receiving thousands of suggestions from citizens all over the country. The designs came in all sizes and colours and ran the gamut from childish scribbles on scrap paper to a beautifully embroidered white satin effort. I recall taking some of them with me on speaking engagements. Although a new flag was not chosen during our years in office, it was pretty clear to me as early as 1957 that there would have to be movement on the issue before too long.

Protocol was also a responsibility of the Secretary of State. Shortly after my arrival in the department, Howard Measures, whose responsibility it was, came to me with a new list of ministers for my approval. On scanning the chart I noticed the right-hand column was headed 'Wives' wherein were listed the wives of cabinet ministers. Sure enough, there was Gordon's name. It did not take me long to seize a pen and cross out 'Wives' and insert 'Spouses.' Mr Measures was amused but said that he regretted that no one had noticed it before it was brought for my approval. It was a good thing that I had a long record as a proofreader and that I caught it at first glance.

When there was a state dinner at Government House, Olive Diefenbaker would have the wives of the Ministers to dine at 24 Sussex Drive. Of course she invited Gordon, who accepted and, resplendent in white tie and tails, joined the others. Gordon had met most of the wives, and they were delighted, hailing him as a 'real trouper,' which he certainly was – not only then but through all my parliamentary career of thirteen years, and in all my activities.

One of the first things I did as Secretary of State was ask my deputy what the program was for celebrating 1 July on Parliament Hill. Any arrangements would be coordinated through my department. He said that, to his knowledge, nothing was planned. He hastened to explain that no one would attend because everyone would be at their summer cottages, hiking in the Gatineau Hills, or vacationing elsewhere. To say that I was shocked is to put it mildly. It was too late to start anything for that year, but I gave orders that plans should proceed forthwith for a celebration the following year. From that beginning has grown the large and enthusiastic celebrations now held on Parliament Hill each 1 July. By Dominion Day 1958 I was no longer Secretary of State, but in my capacity as Minister of Citizenship and Immigration I held Citizenship Court in the foyer directly in front of the entrance to the Chamber of the House of Commons. My successor as Secretary of State, Henri Courtemanche, had the honour of introducing what is now a national event.

The Queen's Printer, Edmund Cloutier, was also probably surprised when I challenged him on the purchase of a printing press. Since Gordon had been a printer almost all his life, he had some knowledge of the industry and I drew upon his expertise. The department had intended to buy the equipment from a firm in New York and presented its order to me for approval. I knew that this equipment was available from a Toronto firm, Toronto Type Foundry, and I refused to sanction the order. I never did find out who had what connections with the American firm, but we had our instructions to support Canadian manufacturers and stop purchases in the United States and elsewhere when a Canadian option was available.

Sensing that we would win a healthy majority, John Diefenbaker called an election for 31 March 1958. It was the easiest campaign of my career. Gordon Churchill spoke at my nominating convention, and I travelled extensively, promoting our cause. On election night, the Progressive Conservatives swept the country, winning 208 of 265 seats. Again I received more votes (nearly 20,000) than my two opponents (Dorothy Crewe for the Liberals and William Scandlan for the CCF) combined.

On 12 May 1958, I was 'promoted' to Citizenship and Immigration. It was a high-profile department that gave me my share of headaches. In addition to running Citizenship and Immigration, the Minister was responsible for Indian Affairs and answered in Parliament for five federal agencies: the Dominion Carillonneur, the National Film Board, the National Gallery, the Public Archives/National Library, and the Royal Canadian Mint. With one glaring exception, these agencies gave me little grief, although I was pestered in the House about details relating to their administration. They were all headed by capable administrators: Robert Donnell was the very talented Carillonneur, Guy Roberge was responsible for the National Film Board, Alan Jarvis headed the National Gallery, and Kaye Lamb was the Dominion Archivist, responsible as well for the National Library.

An incident involving the National Gallery provoked a major controversy early in my tenure at Citizenship and Immigration. While on a buying trip in Europe early in 1957, Alan Jarvis had set his heart on purchasing a painting by Breughel, the famous sixteenth-century painter. Its estimated value was in the range of a half a million dollars. Since there were inadequate funds left in the purchase account of the Gallery, the money to buy the painting had to be secured through a special parliamentary appropriation. When we came to power in June 1957 there was a great furore about the Breughel, because times were particularly bad and unemployment was rising. How could we justify authorizing additional expenditures for an 'old' painting that would only be buried in the National Gallery?

Alan wanted the painting with a passion that clouded his judgment. At the same time as he promised us that he would clear the whole matter up, he apparently made commitments to buy it. I think he rather expected our minority government to fall within a year, after which he would persuade his Liberal friends to pick up the tab. I do not believe that they would have done so, especially after the publicity that had swirled around the purchase. Alan could not see that he had done anything wrong, although he had certainly committed the Canadian government to spend monies that were not available. While it is true that today the painting would be viewed as a sound investment, especially at the price Alan finally negotiated of $350,000, it would have been only an asset for the Gallery and would in no way have helped to balance the budget.

There was really only one solution and that was to fire Alan Jarvis. Had we kept him on, we would certainly have had to honour his commitment, because he was an employee of the state. Threats of lawsuits were mooted from Europe and also through New York. As a result, we were forced to repudiate him, which was too bad. I shall never forget the day he sat in my office waiting for the axe to fall. I told him as carefully and as firmly as I could that I had no choice but to ask for his resignation. 'Very well,' he said, 'but will you give me a little time so that I can break the news to my mother before she hears about it through the media?' I agreed to this request and gave him three weeks, which included the Labour Day weekend of 1959. We parted amicably, and three weeks later, after conferring with him again, we accepted his resignation.

As a result, I received some nasty letters from artists and art lovers across Canada. One in particular, from a great Canadian artist, I very much regretted. The critics were all long on art and short on finance. I wonder how they would have reacted had Alan committed them personally to an expenditure of money they did not have? However, you could not argue with them, so I ignored the protests. All the same, it was a disagreeable situation.

One night the telephone rang in my hotel room at about 3:00 a.m. When I sleepily answered it, an irate voice demanded to know, 'What are you going to do about these Chinese people who are being held here by Immigration officials?' I asked, 'Where?' to which he replied, 'Vancouver.' I informed him that this was my residence, not my office, and he could call the office in the morning. But he wanted an answer 'Now!' Apparently, the people had just arrived. Since there was a three-hour time difference between Vancouver and Ottawa, it was about midnight out there. I told him that I would get the particulars at my office in the morning. 'You mean you don't know about this?' he queried. 'Of course not,' I replied. The next day a Vancouver paper erupted in bold headlines, 'MINISTER KNOWS NOTHING.' After that episode I had the hotel switchboard hold all calls between 11:00 p.m. and 7:00 a.m. I also had my room equipped with a private line for communicating with my family and staff. That way I knew that any calls on that line would not be of a controversial nature.

In the postwar period momentum was developing to change the criteria for immigration to Canada away from country of origin and family relationships and toward individual attributes such as education, skills, and work experience. Such a shift would eliminate to some degree the preference given to immigrants from the United States and western Europe and open the doors to people with employable skills from anywhere in the world. This was a policy that my department supported throughout my years in office and that was embodied in the reform of the immigration regulations, announced in the House in February 1962.

Of course, then as now there was divided opinion within Canada about how many immigrants should be admitted in any given year. This issue became especially topical when a recession descended in 1958. In the minds of many Canadians, immigrants would only add to the number of unemployed chasing scarce jobs. Although those opposed and those in support of an open-door policy seemed just about equal (if the letters sent to my office were any indication), those opposed always seemed to be most vocal. Horror stories were quickly picked up by the media, and my office had to handle the 'damage control.'

The ebb and flow of immigrants to Canada make an interesting study. In the early 1950s there was real concern in Europe that another war might be declared at any moment; consequently the numbers of European immigrants and refugees increased. The numbers dropped in 1958 and remained low until the mid-1960s. I was constantly reminded that the number of new Canadians during my years as Minister was insufficient for the nation's needs. The fact that these were bad years for employment in Canada did not stop the critics. We could never win, whatever we did.

Table 1 shows the trends in immigration in absolute numbers. The pressures respecting immigration policy were constant and of two distinct types. Some people demanded increased numbers for various reasons – humanitarian, economic, political – while others, especially among labour, argued for curtailment, especially during periods of high unemployment. Critics accused the Minister responsible for 'turning the tap off and turning it on again.' There was no 'tap.' Under the regulations the immigrant flow came in, not because a tap was turned on or off but because of circumstances in the country of origin and the perception there as to the opportunities available in Canada. For instance, if the job situation was bad in West Germany we received a large influx of West Germans, but if there was plenty of work there they stayed home. People also stayed home if job prospects were poor in Canada. Political crises, of course, were less predictable than economic conditions, but the propor-

Table 1   Number of immigrants to Canada by year, 1950–1967

1950	73,912	1956	164,857	1962	74,586
1951	194,391	1957	282,164	1963	93,151
1952	164,498	1958	124,851	1964	112,606
1953	168,868	1959	106,928	1965	146,758
1954	154,227	1960	104,111	1966	194,743
1955	109,946	1961	71,689	1967	222,876

tion of refugees in our immigrant population was never large during the late 1950s and early 1960s.

During my years as Minister, Canada supported a program to help clear European refugee camps of tubercular patients. I agreed to meet the first plane load of these refugees and their families at Malton Airport in Toronto. Some were frightened, and all of them were tired from their long journey. It had been arranged that those who were afflicted would be hospitalized, at least until the extent of their ailment had been determined. Living accommodations were provided for the healthy members of their families and, it was hoped, employment for those who were qualified.

One couple was put into a taxi for transportation to the Weston Sanatorium. When they arrived the man kissed his wife goodbye and he went into the San, while she was transported to the apartment provided for them. After a couple of weeks in the hospital, during which time he was subjected to a number of tests, the doctor summoned him to the office and told him that he did not have tuberculosis. 'Yes, I know,' he replied. The man admitted that his wife had TB but maintained that she could not be admitted for treatment because she was the breadwinner in the family! Apparently, they considered the hospital stay a form of penance which either one could perform rather than a required treatment for the victim of the disease.

Generally speaking, the Prime Minister left me to run the department, but in a few cases he interfered by insisting on 'landing' someone who was not acceptable by departmental standards. No matter what the circumstances, he refused to discuss the issue, no doubt because he had been persuaded by individuals or the press that executive action was in order. After tearing large strips of hide off me, he would then demand action forthwith to accommodate the would-be applicant. This behaviour did nothing for the morale of the Minister or her staff.

What made my job particularly difficult was the fact that the Minister had the power to grant exemptions to the rules. As a result, the pressure was intense and constant from many quarters to 'make just one exception.' By December 1959 the Prime Minister began to regret that he had ever interfered with the activities of our department. Once one exception was made, other claimants had good reason to complain about discrimination.

According to my notes, the first week of December 1959 was a nightmare owing to the publicity given to the case of the Chan family. The Chans – husband, wife, and daughter – were from Hong Kong but arrived in Canada from England. When they were denied immigrant status by the department, they turned to the media in an effort to reverse the decision. Mr Chan went into hiding while his wife informed the press that she had sold her engagement ring to raise the funds to enable herself and her young daughter to come to Ottawa to plead their case personally to the Minister. If forced to return to Hong Kong, she claimed, the family would be sentenced to a life of poverty.

Mrs Chan finally came to see me with her daughter in tow, a lovely child about seven years old. Although I am sure that she could speak and understand English, she insisted on her daughter acting as interpreter, which made for a rather stilted interview. I must admit that I was surprised that she could afford to travel by air to Ottawa to plead her case. I was even more startled when she appeared in my office wearing a full-length mink coat over a beautifully embroidered gown and having in her ears two lovely pearls which I estimated to be about 3/8 of an inch in diameter. Poverty indeed!

Perhaps because of the attention that the media devoted to Mrs Chan, two other incidents in that same week threw the office into a tailspin. An Italian gentleman called, insisting that I clear the decks for his cousin to come to Canada. I explained that I could not accede to his wishes because there was a huge backlog in Rome and officials could not clear specific cases ahead of those who were waiting their turn. Then a hysterical Pole called, demanding that I bring out his sister and her medically unfit husband so they could live with his mother who was widowed and living in the Welland-Thorold area. I tried to explain that his brother-in-law could not be allowed to enter Canada unless the provincial authorities sanctioned it (because of the medical problems), but he just wailed and called my attention to his 'poor mother' who was living alone. I asked if she did not have him and he replied, 'Oh, yes, but I can't go to Welland.' When I opined that she might come to Hamilton, he seemed quite shocked and said, 'But she has such a lovely home.'

This was the usual story – one person lands, he brings children or siblings. The next thing we knew, it was Canada's fault that the family was not all together. If we did not permit the entry of all the relatives, even to second cousins once removed, we were guilty of dire discrimination. The problem was particularly acute among Chinese immigrants. Canadians of Chinese ancestry often claimed as a brother or nephew someone whose family connection could not be established. Frequently, it turned out that the proposed immigrant was to be employed in the sponsor's business, most likely as a cook in a restaurant. During my years in office, there was strong evidence of a ring of unscrupulous operators who were exploiting the desperation of prospective Chinese immigrants. We set up an inquiry into the matter, but I never felt that we quite got to the bottom of the problem before I moved on to another portfolio.

We owe a great deal to the people from other countries with diverse customs who have transformed Canada into a multicultural nation, but several years in Immigration made me cynical about the stories used by many people to justify access to Canada. Too often those with real cause for our attention were overlooked because of the smokescreen raised by those who had special access to the media and their political friends.

I am told that a letter was seized from one rascal involved in a Chinese immigration ring indicating that I was a difficult person and nothing could be done as long as I held the Immigration post. However, it went on to say that if Roland Michener were the minister 'things would be different!' 'Rollie' had a large number of Chinese immigrants in his riding, and apparently they thought they could put more pressure on him than they could on me. From one of my memos to the Prime Minister, I also find the following:

December 1961
You may be interested to know that two ethnic press editors talked to me at Al Grosart's as follows:

Editor: We are so glad to see you because you are not at all what we had been told you were like.

Ellen Fairclough: And what were you told?

Ed: Oh, that you were cold and unapproachable and that no one could talk to you.

Ellen: Now, that's interesting and just who would say a thing like that?

1st Ed: (some hesitation) We – ll frankly, some of your own colleagues.

2nd Ed: We're going back to Toronto and tell them it isn't true.

Of course, I thanked them warmly.

One could never be too sure who was for you and who was 'agin' you in the wonderful world of politics.

In 1959, by an Order-in-Council, our government narrowed the range of close relatives who could be sponsored into Canada by residents of non-British background. This controversial measure had been well thrashed out in cabinet. We decided that some action must be taken because of the large number of family-sponsored immigrants arriving without skills of any kind or even the ability to read and write. Once here these unfortunates were often set adrift by their sponsors, many becoming dependent on the state for welfare.

This policy was announced as I went on holidays. When I returned, I found that 'the roof had fallen in.' With a provincial election campaign under way in Ontario, the pressure was fierce. The provincial minister in charge of immigration was raising particular hell. According to his interpretation, the Order was designed to discriminate against Italians in particular, which was not so. He maintained that he could not be re-elected as a Progressive Conservative as long as the Order stood on the books. The media, immigration lawyers, even the Ontario Premier got involved, with the result that Diefenbaker demanded that the Order be rescinded. Of course, yours truly got the blame, and there was plenty of it. That was the first time that I nearly resigned.

Subsequently, I received a visit from the Italian Minister responsible for emigration from his country. We tried to explain to him the problems that arose when immigrants to Canada could neither read nor write. His solution was quite simple: the government of Canada should set up schools in Italy to teach the intended immigrants to read, write, and speak English. I nearly fell off my chair at this magnificent piece of presumption. After I regained my composure, I pointed out that we had trouble finding funds to educate our own citizens, let alone establish schools abroad. Such a plan would never be sanctioned by the tax-paying electorate.

Although unfortunately I did not keep a diary, except for appointments, occasionally I would type a few notes on my machine in my hotel room. The following is undated, but it recounts events in 1960:

I thought it would happen and it has! For months now we have been planning a trip to European offices. This was the trip which had to be postponed from 1958 (when I went to the UK only) and from 1959 when the whole trip was cancelled on an itinerary which had been carefully worked out to put it into four weeks covering Netherlands, Belgium, Denmark (with Scandinavian officers to meet me there), Germany (Bonn, Cologne, Berlin), Austria, Italy, and France. Officers from Spain, Portugal, and Greece were to meet me in Rome. Thus I would cover the whole of Europe on the continent and then spend two days in London.

Last Monday I received a note from the P.M. saying that although he had told me in April to do this trip in the autumn, he now felt the time was inopportune because of the imminence of cabinet changes. Ottawa, of course, has been full of the rumoured shuffle for weeks and I just heard on the same day (Monday) that I was probably to be included and the grapevine had it that I would be shuffled into Health and Welfare. I didn't believe it but you never know.

Thursday I had a nine o'clock appointment with the P.M. and awoke with a throbbing headache – something I rarely have but this is a beaut. I arrived, headache and all, to hear that I was to cancel the trip but not a word about cabinet changes. However, he did say that I had the worst department in government (he is telling me!) but went on to say that my personal popularity across the country was great and wherever he went he got glowing accounts of it. He then said that he wanted me to go across the country and speak wherever I could. This is easy to arrange because I have ten times the number of invitations I can ever accept and it only involves accepting a few.

So that is that! I can't say I'm sorry although I feel at a distinct disadvantage administratively when I have never even seen the overseas offices of my own department.

The Canadian trip will be just as rugged if not more so because the press is a constant hazard but I will take Kingsley Brown along and, if I can manage it with a private car, I will probably take Willi Gallagher also.

For reasons that are cloaked in much secrecy, the cabinet shuffle turned out to be a minor affair that did not affect my portfolio at all. I still have not had my European tour!

Another problem in Immigration concerned children born in Canada to immigrant parents who were subsequently deported. In some instances, the parents had been in Canada for several years without status. When it came time to deport them, the children went with their parents. The children remained Canadian citizens because they had been born in Canada.

In 1959 Jack Pickersgill, who had preceded me in the department, started to ask questions about specific cases that alerted me to the possibility that, when the Estimates of the department were being debated, I might expect the subject to be discussed at some length. Accordingly, I instructed my staff to prepare a list of all such cases during the incumbency of my predecessor. I kept this information in my office in the House so that I could get it at short notice. Sure enough, when the Estimates were being considered, the subject arose, and before the honourable gentleman resumed his seat I had the list in my hands. In *Hansard* I am quoted thus: 'I am very pleased to learn the Hon. gentleman now has a real concern for the children of immigrants. I have in my hand some cases in which deportation was ordered and in which there were Canadian children involved.' I then went on to cite particulars. For instance, 'A citizen of Haiti entered Canada as a student and took employment. There was an application for a landing permit and he was ordered deported at Toronto on December 2, 1954, the wife included. The appeal was dismissed ... and the Canadian child accompanied the parents.' Mr Pickersgill graciously replied, 'The hon. lady has me there, I admit.' Of course, he then argued that just because he had done it did not mean it was right, although what he would have me do was difficult to determine.

In another case, a family was emigrating to Canada from Ireland when their young daughter was stricken with an epileptic seizure. She was henceforth ruled inadmissible to Canada. The matter was brought to my attention. It appeared that this was the first such attack, but departmental regulations were such that the only advice we could give was that she should return to Ireland to live with relatives. In this case I intervened and gave instructions that she should be allowed to land with her family. The treatment of epilepsy has undergone major advances since that time. Now, victims of the ailment are not ostracized as was formerly the case and are able to lead normal lives, thanks to medical science. In fact, my own son, Howard, became a victim of epilepsy after he was forty years old. When Howard's illness was diagnosed, I immediately thought of the little Irish girl and was thankful that I had decided in her favour. I should add that Howard's case was manageable with proper medication.

In addition, the department was always being blamed for favouring immigration to certain areas of the country, but the reality was that we had no control over where immigrants finally settled. Every month we issued a guide for the overseas offices, listing employment opportunities in various regions of Canada. However, if an electrician destined for Winnipeg decided to live in Toronto because his friends were there we were in no position to force him to move to his stated destination. Since many immigrants had little idea of the size of the country, they often had wildly impractical ideas about where they could live and work until they actually arrived in Canada.

We also got blamed for refusing to offer landed immigrant status to students who were sponsored by their home countries to study in Canada. By the conditions of their scholarships, these students were required to return home and share the benefits of their education with their own people. However, a few of them got a taste of Canada and conveniently forgot their commitment. Once the applicant got the ear of the press, the case was usually presented as one in which a highly qualified individual was being rejected because of racial origins or some other attribute, which implied that we were prejudiced in our decision making. That, of course, was not the reason at all, but that was the image left with the public by the press.

It is true that Citizenship and Immigration was a terrible department to administer. One of the reasons that it came into such disrepute was the lack of a good, firm policy. I tried for months after assuming the portfolio to get the cabinet to consider my suggestions for reform, but I was brushed off – so many other things were considered more important. I also found my Deputy Minister difficult to deal with. Although we got along on a personal basis, he was a rigid man, used to military discipline, who would stubbornly resist my efforts to introduce change in departmental policy. He would argue until I just had to thump the desk and say, 'Look, this is the way it's going to be.' Then he would relent and say, 'Oh, well, all right, if you say so,' but in the meantime I had wasted two hours in frustrating debate. (Indian Affairs was different. It too had a man of military background as the Director, but if I said that I wanted something done he would bend over backwards to do it.)

Following the problems we experienced in 1959, I knew that something had to be done to improve the department's image. I told Diefenbaker that I wanted a new deputy minister and suggested Dr George Davidson, then a deputy at Health and Welfare. I do not think that he relished the move, but as a good civil servant he accepted his new assignment with grace, and it was a happy day for me when George joined the department.

George was born in Bass River, Nova Scotia, in 1911. His mother died shortly after he was born. Following the First World War, George, his brother, and their invalid father moved to the west coast to live with three maiden aunts, who took turns retiring from their jobs as teachers to take care of their new charges. George did well in school, took a BA from the University of British Columbia in 1928, and graduated from Harvard with a PhD in Classics in 1932. Since university positions were hard to come by during the Depression, he found work in public welfare in British Columbia. He subsequently followed Charlotte Whitton as Executive Director of the Canadian Welfare Council in 1942. Two years later he joined the federal civil service as one of the Deputy Ministers in Health and Welfare. Associated with the implementation of Family Allowances, Old Age Pensions, and Hospital Insurance, Dr Davidson brought valuable experience in social service and public relations to my department.

George was an exceptional person who stood firm on principle – I could never budge him on a matter of principle – but was flexible in administrative matters. He had a wonderful sense of humour and could always see the other person's point of view. Under the pressure of events we used to write little notes on the margins of documents, and some of these comments were quite amusing. George warned me that some day researchers would dig out the files and wonder just what kind of people we were to write such things. I wonder if these documents have survived the pruning that now occurs in the National Archives?

With George Davidson's help, our government was able in 1962 to bring in new immigration regulations, which at least marked the beginning of reform. Essentially we were attempting to make education, training, and skills the primary criteria for immigration, rather than family relationship and country of origin. At the same time we expanded the scope of the immigration appeal board so that all potential deportees had the opportunity for an independent hearing. While the Opposition criticized us for substituting one set of discriminatory regulations for another, the new direction was consistent with the principles of the Bill of Rights (1960) and was the same basis on which the Liberals reformed the Immigration Act in 1967.

Because immigration is such an emotionally charged issue, people working in my department were sometimes in physical danger. On one occasion, Joe Bissett, an immigration officer attached to the Minister's office, reported to me that he was having considerable trouble with a landed immigrant from Yugoslavia. The man apparently wanted his sister to apply for landed immigrant status, but she would not do so unless her husband could also come to Canada. There were some irregularities in his application, and his admission naturally had to be refused. This decision threw him into a rage. He told Joe, 'I will come into your office and bring a big knife. I will cut my throat and the blood will be all over your desk.' Joe's flippant reply was, 'Don't do it here. Go up to Admissions on the fourth floor.' Naturally such levity was lost on the applicant. He continued to threaten Joe during the course of a couple of visits to our offices. Joe thought it amusing, but I pointed out that, although it was unlikely, it was quite possible that he would attempt to carry out his threat. I asked George Davidson to consult with us. He argued that the threat could not be ignored. Consequently, on the next appointment, two RCMP officers were installed out of sight in an adjoining room, with the door open.

The man came in and laid a large knife on the desk in front of Joe and repeated his threat. Joe said, in a loud voice, 'Put that knife away.' There was no response from the police. Joe repeated his warning, but it was only after his third utterance that the officers finally intervened. In the meantime, there was plenty of time for him to have killed Joe and himself. Apparently, the officers were waiting for a definitive move on the part of the man. He was eventually arrested and charged. The brother-in-law did NOT get into Canada.

Another time when Gordon was with me in Ottawa, we were having breakfast in our room when I responded to a knock on the door to find an RCMP officer, who informed me that he had been assigned to guard me that day because a certain would-be immigrant was in Ottawa and had threatened my life. I was not much impressed, because, after all, what could he gain by such action? Certainly he could not get what he wanted – that is, landed immigrant status – if I were dead. Gordon was intrigued by the way the officer dogged my footsteps all day long. When I left my office for meetings or attendance in the House, he followed. For the rest of the time, he sat on a chair outside my office door.

The increase in immigration after the Second World War warranted the creation of a system of Citizenship Courts to serve new Canadians. When I assumed responsibility for Citizenship and Immigration, there were Citizenship Courts only in Toronto and Montreal. In all other localities, applicants for citizenship were forced to appear before a judge in the regular courts, along with other litigants. After sitting through a criminal case, many immigrants must have felt like criminals themselves.

I determined to set up as many courts as possible and began with my own city of Hamilton. It was set up exactly to my liking. The President of the Court (now called a 'judge') was B.W. (Beamer) Hopkins, QC, a former Magistrate, who gave up a much higher-paying job for this one. The Clerk of the court was Laura Arnold. Hers was a Civil Service appointment, which had to go through the mill of application, examination, and competition. By 1982 there were thirty-four Courts of Canadian Citizenship across the country, and I am glad to have started the ball rolling.

Not long after the Hamilton Citizenship Court was established, I learned that some of the other MPs in Hamilton felt that I had not sufficiently consulted them with respect to the appointments. When Diefenbaker informed me that Quinto Martini had complained that Hopkins had been appointed without his being consulted, my immediate reaction was, 'Why should I?' but fortunately I bit my tongue. Meanwhile, I set up a Court in London and made plans for another in Vancouver. I asked Howard Green to name a President for the Vancouver Court, and he came up with the name of Eric Chown. When the Order-in-Council was presented to the Prime Minister for signing, he asked if I had consulted with all of the Ministers from British Columbia. I said 'No,' but that I had consulted with the Secretary of State for External Affairs, in whose city the court was located. I said, further, that this was my usual practice and that if it had been a Victoria Court I would have consulted George Pearkes, or if in the interior of the province Davie Fulton. Then I made the mistake of saying that I had appointed the Court at Hamilton, whereupon he jumped on me with both feet: 'Yes, and you didn't even consult with your local members on that one, and there has been trouble ever since.' Of course there was no trouble at all. That was just his usual exaggeration.

There was a small triumph in the appointment of Laura Arnold to the Hamilton Citizenship Court. Although I did not suffer greatly from discrimination because of my sex, Laura had been the object of outrageous treatment by misguided corporate executives. While employed in a firm that manufactured paper milk cartons, she had risen to be Secretary-Treasurer. The company had prospered and had eventually been taken over by Continental Can. Shortly thereafter, one of its officials had gone to Laura's office and said, 'Sorry, Mrs Arnold, but the policy of this company is no women executives. However, we are willing to put you in charge of Accounts Payable.' Laura had refused to accept the demotion and had left.

The result of this shock was that she had lost her self-confidence as well as her job. While she was adjusting, I had employed her in my own office, and she had subsequently taken a position with Chagnon and MacGillivray, Chartered Accountants, where her services had been highly praised. When I was setting up the Citizenship Court, I thought of Laura and encouraged her to apply for the position of Clerk. She was loath to do so, but I urged her to go ahead. Because it was a Civil Service appointment, I had little influence over the selection process but I knew that she was well qualified. One day an official of my department came into the office and asked, 'Who is this woman who has applied to be Clerk of the Court in Hamilton? Do you know her?' I conceded that I did, and he informed me that she was so much more qualified than the other applicants that the senior officers in the department proposed to appoint her. Since it was my home territory, they had felt obliged to inform me, in case the appointment was inappropriate in some way. Needless to say, I was delighted to be able to say, 'I told you so.' Laura served the Court with dignity and competence until her mandatory retirement. As the first woman to hold such a position, she received some much-deserved publicity in the local press.

Despite what people think, one really has very little scope for patronage as a Minister of the Crown. I could appoint people to my office staff and presidents of Citizenship Courts but most positions came under the jurisdiction of the Civil Service Commission. I think this is as it should be, but it was difficult convincing constituents that I did not have the power to make their dreams come true. It was the same situation with government contracts. Although one might intervene at the Treasury Board level to make sure that the company with the better track record was awarded the contract, it was difficult to demand that a contract be awarded on a purely partisan basis. In my constituency, Progressive Conservative businessmen groused because they failed to receive preference, but there was a limit to what I could and would do in this regard.

Indian Affairs was also under the jurisdiction of the Department of Citizenship and Immigration. Given the complexity of the issues relating to Aboriginal peoples, Indian Affairs could well have been a separate portfolio, but it was not. The Native peoples were beginning to find a political voice in the 1950s. Indeed, our government helped to strengthen that voice. Diefenbaker appointed Akay-na-muka, also known by his English name, James Gladstone, as Canada's first Indian Senator in February 1958. Two years later I had the privilege of introducing legislation into the House that would give status Indians the right to vote in federal elections. Although some Native leaders feared that enfranchisement was a device to undermine their treaty rights, I made it very clear that this was not the case. No Indian, or any Canadian, is forced to vote, but it is a privilege that every Canadian citizen has a right to exercise.

As Minister responsible for Indian Affairs, I visited as many reserves as possible, probably as many as a hundred of the more than five hundred that can be found in Canada. I was always received with the utmost courtesy and often received requests for action on matters of particular concern. Sometimes it was possible to accede to their demands immediately; in others, I agreed to carry the problem back to my colleagues. It was easy to approach the Prime Minister on Indian affairs, because he was their great champion – so much so that he invariably spoke in the House on issues important to them, relegating the responsible Minister to a secondary role. I am sure that the Indians were complimented and pleased, even if the Minister was not. Indeed, in all honesty, I cannot find fault, because I probably would have done the same in his circumstances.

I enjoyed the pomp and ceremony associated with my visits to reserves and several events stand out particularly in my mind. While on a visit to a reserve in Manitoba, I was able to grant one of the requests made to me. Although I arrived late, those within earshot returned to the school-house, which was the location for our diplomatic exchange. After the usual pleasantries the Chief, who was quite young, introduced his father, who had been Chief before him. Everything had to be translated to the former Chief, even though he and we knew that he understood every word and could have joined the discussion in English. However, it was a matter of pride and protocol, one that we all respected.

I asked the Chief if there were any problems, and he mentioned a few that we promised to take under advisement. Then he brought up the 'missionary,' a woman who represented one of the major churches and lived a short distance from the school where we had gathered. According to the Chief she interfered in everything – even to the extent of going into classrooms and contradicting the teacher. Apparently she and a female companion would drive down the dirt road of the reserve at a speed that would generate a great cloud of dust. Even as he said it, she came along to prove his point. Seeing a crowd in the school yard, she turned around and stopped a short distance away. She beckoned some of the women to approach her car and asked them what was going on. When she found out that it was a visit from the Minister, she reluctantly drove away – at a reduced speed.

The Chief maintained that getting rid of 'that *** missionary' was the top priority among the problems that we had discussed. On returning to Ottawa, we got in touch with the church involved and succeeded in getting her removed from that post. A couple of years later, at a meeting with the provincial authorities concerning welfare matters among the Indians and Métis, this young Chief came up to me, shook my hand, and said, 'Thanks.'

Another visit that stands out in my mind is the one to the Peigan Reserve in Brocket, Alberta. The band there had expressed the wish to invest me as an Honorary Chief, but it was explained to them that the Minister could not accept the honour while still in office. Instead, it arranged an Indian prayer ceremony, which took place inside an enormous tepee with hangings on the walls and rugs spread on the ground. In the centre, inside a circle of stones, glowed a small fire. I was asked to sit among several of their elegantly robed leaders, who, from time to time, threw herbs like incense on the small fire. The tepee was fragrant with the herbal aroma. They joined in prayers for my safe journey and good health. For some reason this ceremony was especially touching, and I treasure the memory.

At the other end of the country, it was my great pleasure to present almost $4000 to three Micmac students during a visit to Eskasoni in Cape Breton. Indian Affairs had educational programs that gave many bright young Indians an opportunity to expand their horizons. Another time, I was presented with a pair of matched mink pelts by Mr Burton Jacobs, Chief of the Walpole Band in Ontario, who attended a Rotary Club luncheon at which I was the guest speaker. I was later told that he had hunted a whole season to find such a perfectly matched pair of pelts.

After I left Citizenship and Immigration, I received a number of honours from Native groups across the country. In September 1962 I attended the 13th Annual Six Nations Pageant, where I received the name Au Wa Ha Da Go, which means 'Bright Flower.' In a colourful and moving ceremony at Gleichen, Alberta, in December 1962, the Blackfoot made me an Honorary Chief of the Sik'Sika, naming me Pe Ta Ke ('Eagle Woman') after a female chief who lived many years ago. Blackfoot Chief Ed Axe said that I, as Minister responsible for Indian Affairs, had taken a lively interest in the welfare of Native peoples and was the only Minister who had ever seen the Indians as human. It was kind of him to say so.

Indian Affairs was at once intriguing and frustrating because of the large number of individual bands. Their problems covered a wide range of conditions, and even in a single band there were quite distinct differences of opinion as to the solution to any given problem. This is true for any group of citizens, but in my day there was a growing gulf between Indians who claimed to be traditionalists and those who wished to be more actively integrated into the broader Canadian scene. This differing approach to government would be dramatically exposed in 1969, when the Trudeau government issued its now infamous White Paper on Indian Affairs. In my time as Minister responsible for Indian Affairs, the issue mostly percolated beneath the surface. However, the same could not be said for our government, which by 1962 was being openly attacked from a number of directions.

7

Dark Days: The Bitter End

My patience was wearing thin as I approached my fifth year as a cabinet minister. And most of my colleagues felt the same way. With 208 caucus members to satisfy, and difficult issues of national policy to resolve, there seemed to be no prospect of respite from the constant demands of public office. In March 1962 the Prime Minister accused me of being curt with him when he called to ask me to do something. He hinted that I could be replaced, and I replied, 'Well, that suits me fine, if that's the way you want it,' and hung up. Diefenbaker called right back and demanded that I meet him in his office. Apparently he was seldom talked to that way, and obviously he did not like it. I explained that I was a business person and often was impatient on the phone, but he considered my curtness that particular day as a personal affront to him, and I left his office even more angry than when I went in. Once back in my office I began to calm down. We were all pretty edgy under the pressure of government, and if it had been a bad week for me it had probably been a bad week for him too.

The frustrations of political life sometimes became intolerable, but my good friend Gordon Churchill taught me a valuable lesson when on one occasion I threatened to throw in the towel. In urging me to reconsider my hasty decision, he said words to this effect: 'Who do you think you are? After all we are all experiencing these frustrations; you are no different from the rest of us.' I thought to myself, 'That's right! Who do I think I am that I can't put up with this stuff?' And so I did put up with it, and stuck it out to the bitter end.

In the winter of 1962 things were going from bad to worse. We were facing an election, and the public mood was not as favourable to us as it had been in 1958. The Social Credit Party was picking up support in the west under Robert Thompson and was even managing to make inroads in Quebec under its dynamic leader, Réal Caouette. Social Credit had little appeal in Hamilton, but the New Democratic Party was another matter. Building on its CCF foundations, it formed close ties with organized labour and set out under its popular leader, Tommy Douglas, to succeed where its predecessor had failed. The Liberals were also poised to recapture the power they were convinced they should never have lost.

While it may be true that our large majority made it difficult to develop an efficient government, it was probably the devaluation of the dollar and the confusion that surrounded that issue in the media that contributed to the loss of so many seats in 1962. The decision in February to peg the dollar at 92 cents was one I supported and I still feel was a wise one administratively, but it was difficult to sell to the public, especially those who lived close to the American border and found their purchasing power decrease overnight. The international 'run' on the Canadian dollar did not help matters either. In later years Canadians became more accustomed to the pressure that international financial structures place on national economies, but in 1962 the whole issue got caught up in the election campaign, much to our discredit.

Since my organization was less than perfect, I had to fight an uphill battle in my own riding. Although I managed to squeak through, I was not thrilled with the slim margin in my favour. The final tally looked like this: Ellen Fairclough (PC) 12,794; Balys Kronas (Liberal) 11,047; Gary Chertkoff (NDP) 5,321; and Alfred Dewhurst (Communist) 421. At the national level we were left to manage a minority government, with only 116 of 265 seats. This result marked the beginning of the end for our government and ushered in a period of dark days.

In the cabinet shuffle following the 1962 election, I was transferred to the portfolio of Postmaster General and sworn into office on 9 August. It was somewhat less demanding than Citizenship and Immigration but had no less a high profile. Virtually everyone in the country used the mail system and felt compelled to tell the minister when it failed to perform to their satisfaction. I hoped that my administrative skills might be used to good advantage.

The biggest job facing my new department was a review of our procedures, with the goal of increasing efficiency and decreasing costs. This policy came as a result of the Royal Commission on Government Organization and Finances chaired by Grant Glassco. In order to avoid traps set by the Opposition, I asked my Deputy Minister, Mr Wilson, to have someone research my speeches while in Opposition to see what I had then said about the Post Office. He subsequently sent me a memorandum which read as follows:

Postmaster General Ellen Fairclough should be happy with at least two of the recommendations in Volume III of the Royal Commission on Government Organization. She made them herself when she was an opposition postal critic in 1954.

The Report recommended that the Government Departments be charged for postal service now provided free by the Post Office.

The Report also recommended that the Post Office be charged for office space now provided by the Department of Public Works. This would help indicate the true revenue and expenditure position of the Post Office.

I still think it only proper that the cost-paying department should be credited for any services or space provided to another department. No department should enjoy a 'freebie' at the expense of another. If this rule is not followed, the annual Estimates, which are debated so thoroughly in the House, do not give a true picture of the financial operations of the department concerned. This is now the practice, I understand.

While things remained reasonably calm at the departmental level, the general atmosphere in cabinet and caucus was, to say the least, stormy. The financial crisis, precipitated by the nearly unprecedented drain on the Canadian dollar, and our minority position in the House made it difficult to pursue creative policies. Austerity was the watchword, and we were all hamstrung by the funding cutbacks demanded by the Department of Finance, under George Nowlan's guiding hand. As we struggled to cope with these problems, we were thrown into a tailspin by the Cuban Missile Crisis, which erupted on 22 October.

Canada's relationship with the United States had changed in the years since the Second World War. By the 1960s the United States had replaced Great Britain as the world's greatest power and Canada had become increasingly dependent, both economically and militarily, on its neighbour to the south. Predictably, there were those, including a number of highly placed people in the business community, who criticized this new world order. Americans, they argued, kept Canadians 'hewers of wood and drawers of water,' and required us to fall into line with their aggressive Cold War policies. Such concerns were raised when we cancelled the Avro Arrow in February 1959 and came back to haunt us during the Cuban Missile Crisis.

When the Americans discovered that the Soviet Union was installing missiles in Cuba, President John F. Kennedy demanded that they be removed; he called on Canada, as a signatory to the North American Air Defence Agreement (NORAD), to put its forces in a state of alert. This precipitated a crisis in our cabinet, because the Secretary of State for External Affairs, Howard Green, was determined not to give in to such sabre-rattling, while the Minister of National Defence, Doug Harkness, was anxious that Canada not be perceived as a reluctant ally. Although the crisis was resolved rather quickly when the Soviet Union backed down, the larger question of whether Canada would adopt nuclear warheads for its new weapons systems suddenly rose to the top of the cabinet agenda.

The atmosphere of crisis was compounded by the emergency measures taken to protect the cabinet in the event bombs began to fall. This was the era of the 'Diefenbunker,' and each cabinet minister had special instructions as to where to go and what to do in the event of war. On the weekend following Kennedy's announcement of the blockade of Cuba, I went home convinced that it might be the last time I would see my family. Yet, because of cabinet secrecy, I could not explain to Gordon and Howard what was happening. Indeed, I did not know myself. The same situation was reflected in the families of all members of the cabinet. It was a terribly tense time for all of us. I am scarcely exaggerating when I say that in the wake of the Cuban crisis we had twenty-three members of the cabinet with incipient nervous breakdowns.

Defence was not my portfolio or my area of expertise, and I therefore tended to go along with the cabinet consensus on matters relating to defence policy. Unfortunately, neither the cabinet nor the Canadian public was in the mood to develop a consensus on nuclear weapons. I felt that Howard Green was being overly idealistic, but it was also the case that Harkness was having difficulty developing an objective perspective on defence policy. Cabinet meetings about nuclear weapons absorbed most of our energies, so that little of a positive nature was accomplished, and everyone began meeting in private offices, trying to figure out a way of resolving the impasse.

As we lurched toward disaster, the Prime Minister, as he was wont to do, asked us to put our policy suggestions on paper. The following from me, dated 8 January 1963, is the result of one of his requests:

In reply to your request this morning, I believe our approach for the next five years should be one of positive and confident expansion in all fields of national endeavour.

We cannot march forward unless we march together. It is the old story, 'United we stand – divided we fall!' Unless all sections of this nation pull together we cannot achieve our goals. To this end, I believe a good start would be the implementation of your suggestion of a Royal Commission on the Great National Purpose. This would encompass Canadianism in all its positive aspects, the welding together of all sections of Canada and all Canadians of whatever race, colour or creed.

One of our goals should be a continuation and acceleration of your own programme of utilization of resources with emphasis not only on natural resources but on economic, industrial, and human resources as well. Much of this is already in prospect under the various Commissions which have been charged with inquiry into specific fields (National productivity, Atlantic provinces, etc.) In this field of utilization of human resources, I think we could consider again some programme of university scholarships.

All of this could be aimed at Centennial – 1967, and be developed as an overall plan to commemorate Canada's Centennial of Confederation – 3 C's. The bricks of this structure are the people themselves, the mortar is the good will of each toward the other, the edifice will be Canada – 1967, a monument to the past, a hope for the future, and a repository for our resources and our culture.

Sounds rather high-flown but I think something along these lines could be made to stick!

With reference to Suburbia, I think the university scholarships would have quite an appeal because the suburbs are homes of young people rearing young families.

There is one practical thing we could do and I think it should be done right away. You will recall I brought up the matter of letter carrier service in adjacent areas (suburbs) to those not now served. Although all of our colleagues supported the suggestion that this should be done as soon as possible, it has been held up by Treasury and Finance. We are getting more bad publicity from this than anything I have seen in a long time. So far it has not broken out into the open but I am receiving letters from individuals, Chambers of Commerce, Mayors, and Members of Parliament complaining bitterly over the lack of service. I can't say I blame them since this is a service which Government is supposed to give – they pay for it and, in my opinion, they are entitled to it.

A complicating factor (not known outside the Department) is that I expect this Department will have a sizable surplus (over $6,000,000) and I don't see how I can explain the lack of service in face of this surplus. In addition, I am sure the postal employees will scream all the louder for wage adjustments when they get this news.

I recognize that Finance would like to lay hands on this money but I think we are just asking for trouble if we don't proceed AT ONCE with the new and extended Letter Carrier walks.

Enclosed is a short explanatory memo from my Deputy which I presented to Cabinet, together with an up-to-date schedule of 'deferred projects.' If you want to please Suburbia, give them mail service – if you want to get them up in arms, withhold it!

Such musings had little effect, as the nuclear weapons issue increasingly called into question Diefenbaker's leadership ability. Although there were rumours – which have subsequently been more or less confirmed – to the effect that some cabinet ministers were involved in a cabal to oust Diefenbaker, I was not privy to, nor would I have supported, such behaviour. I was, of course, present at cabinet and caucus meetings, and I attended the now-famous meeting of ministers at Diefenbaker's home on Sunday morning, 3 February, when we met to discuss whether we should call an election before facing almost certain defeat in the House. The tension in the room was so thick you could cut it with a knife. When Harkness erupted in a statement that essentially called into question his confidence in the Prime Minister, pandemonium ensued. Diefenbaker suddenly stood up and asked those who were with him to stand also. I stood up, concerned that the government not fall because of personality conflicts. In the end, it mattered little what we did that day. We failed to form a firm alliance with the Social Credit Party, whose support we needed to survive, and that was reflected in a vote in the House on 5 February 1963 in which we were defeated 142 to 111.

Despite our rather ignominious end, I take pride in a number of policies advanced by our three governments, including the granting of voting rights to status Indians and the revision of the immigration regulations in which I had a hand. At a general level, I think the Bill of Rights was a step in the right direction. Personally, I got the most pleasure out of cutting through 'red tape,' which, as a Minister, I was occasionally able to do.

I never worked as hard as I did in the 1962 and 1963 campaigns. Because of my position as the only woman in the cabinet, I was called upon to speak all over the country in 1962 and I appeared only briefly in my own constituency. Speaking engagements numbered as many as fourteen in three days. There was little time for sleep. Fortunately, I have always been strong physically, so I did not really mind the pace. In fact, I found it exhilarating, but I knew what the result would be of my long absences from Hamilton West.

My itinerary in the three weeks prior to the 1962 election looked like this:

June 2   Saturday, 3:00 p.m. Muncey Reserve, Middlesex West (Bill Thomas)

June 3   2:00 p.m. Puslinch, Sunset Villa, Danish Constitution Day (guest speaker)

June 4   Monday CLOSE OF NOMINATIONS

June 5   Tuesday Moncton, Prince Edward Island, Summerside
2:30 p.m. Princes Constituency (Dr. Phillips)
9:00 p.m. Montague (Mrs. MacDonald)

June 6   Wednesday Cape Breton, Nova Scotia
2:00 p.m. Sydney (Bob Muir)
3:00 to 5:00 Tour Whitney Pier, Louisbourg
6:30 p.m. TV interview
Visit Micmac reserve
8:00 p.m. New Waterford

June 7   Thursday, 10:00 a.m. Left Sydney for Fredericton
3:00 p.m. Oromocto for meeting and tea
9:00 p.m. Millville

June 8   Friday Met Paul Comtois in Fredericton
9:55 a.m. Fredericton to Malton, arriving 2:30 for Hamilton
8:00 p.m. HMCS *Star* for reception and Hamilton Admiralty Ball at Patriot

June 9   Saturday, 9:00 a.m. Boy Scout parade with Paul Comtois and Lieutenant-Governors of Quebec and Ontario

1:00 p.m. Luncheon, Tamahaac Club

6:30 p.m. Marconi Mutual Benefit Society, annual dinner

June 10 Sunday, 3:00 p.m. Reception at Goodrow residence, Hamilton

June 11 Monday At home writing three five-minute speeches

June 12 Tuesday, 3:00 p.m. Hamilton Women's Tea and Reception
5:00 (Hon. George Hees)

June 13 Wednesday, 10:30 am Conference at HQ re publicity
3:00 p.m. Niagara Falls, open new National Biscuit Co. plant
(Dick Pollock, pres.)

June 14 Thursday, 1:00 p.m. Hired private plane (Reg Spence) to go
Chatham for PC rally (Harold Danforth)
10:00 a.m. Met with Baltic groups in Hamilton

June 15 Friday, 8:00 p.m. Diefenbaker meeting at Palace Theatre, Hamilton (arrangements took most of the day)

June 16 Saturday, 12:15 p.m. Hillfield School
3:00 p.m. Social reception (Doug Dingle for Mary Lou)

June 17 Sunday, 5:00 p.m. Meeting and dinner with Agro

June 18 Monday ELECTION DAY

June 19 Tuesday Flew to Ottawa and had cabinet meetings every day,
including Sunday, to the 28th June.

My last stand for Parliament was made on 8 April 1963. I stuck closer to
home in this campaign but still had a gruelling schedule.

It is one of the perils of public life that one's tongue frequently is responsible for one's misfortunes. At my nomination meeting in 1963, I allowed
myself to get carried away and boldly boasted that we would not allow the
constituency to 'fall into alien hands.' I used words to indicate 'other than
Progressive Conservative,' but they were interpreted by many in the audience, and certainly by my opponents, to mean 'other than Canadian born.'
Since Hamilton was increasingly becoming an immigrant city, and two of
my opponents were of non–Anglo Saxon ancestry, the interpretation was
very damaging to my campaign. But it was done, and there was nothing I
could do about it. I likely could not have won the 1963 election in any
event, but it stung a little that such a small incident could be distorted and
then magnified to such a degree.

As a result of the publicity given to my comment, the switchboard operator at the central police station got an anonymous call on 28 February warning that 'Ellen Fairclough's house is going to be burned tonight.' I was attending a fund-raising banquet for the Hamilton Goodwill Africa Foundation at the Scottish Rite Cathedral. John Campanaro, Vice-President of Westinghouse, and his wife, Maria, came back to our home after the event. When we drew near we were surprised to see a police car in the driveway and another on the street. When we went in we found our son's fiancée, Jeannine Gaudet, with a policeman in attendance. Gordon and Howard had not yet returned from their meeting at the Masonic Lodge. We soon learned that Jeannine had been quite shocked by the arrival of the police, but we were not too worried. I always operate on the assumption that people do not issue warnings if they really intend to do anything drastic.

I said as much to the police and added that I did not think there was any need for surveillance. The officer was very sensible about it. He argued that, although the person probably did not intend any further action, the warning had gone over the air and some crank might think it was a good idea and carry out the threat made by another. The policeman was no doubt right to be careful. The police kept an eye on things for the period prior to the election, which was certainly the roughest campaign in which I was ever involved.

It became clear soon after the polls had closed on 8 April that I would not win, and within less than two hours I conceded. In the final count I was defeated by the thirty-two-year-old Liberal candidate, Joseph Macaluso, by over 2,500 votes. I lost in all sections of the riding, including Westdale, which had always given me strong support. Although my detractors suggested that I was the author of my own defeat, I had for company the other Progressive Conservative candidates in Hamilton, which like most cities in Ontario swung to the Liberals and the NDP. The results were as follows: Joseph Macaluso (Liberal), 13,701; Ellen Fairclough (PC), 10,894; Gary Chertkoff (NDP), 5,709; James Ian Buchan (Social Credit), 442; and Harry Hunter (Communist), 283.

As a common courtesy, I stopped by the headquarters of the winning candidate to offer congratulations. Mr Macaluso was very gracious, but the atmosphere was tense. To my great surprise, I was faced with a huge cartoon depicting me in a most unflattering way and bearing the caption: 'The Witch Is Dead.' I pretended not to notice, but it was difficult. Unfortunately, I did not get a copy of this interesting piece of art for my cartoon collection!

One letter I received following my defeat touched me greatly, and I have kept it in my files. It was from George Nowlan, the MP from Digby-Annapolis-Kings. George was a fair and able man, with a nice mixture of conservative and liberal leanings. When he returned to Ottawa after the election, he thought about his 'fallen' colleagues and scrawled me this note, dated 9 May 1963:

This place is one of broken hearts, broken hopes, and broken offices. Everything is in a mess, and it is all the more desolate because you are not here. Some bright lad got the idea of redecorating all the offices after Election Day. You can imagine the confusion trying to get ready for the 16th. You will remember Rochon in charge of equipment, etc. I heard him cursing Caron (Lib Whip) saying, 'Yesterday we moved 20 Liberals and now find 18 are in the wrong rooms.'

...

The door will always be open to you, but we will probably have Dewars instead of your favourite brand! Seriously, Ellen, we miss you terribly and will never be the same without your breezy personality and gay laughter. However, I suppose we should be thankful for the years we had together. We had fun and work and sometimes tears, and then what should have been happy days were misery. However, the group shared them together, and if history is properly written, our grandchildren can be very proud of the part their grandparents played in the Gov't of Canada.

All the best my dear and come see us soon.

My defeat was not altogether unexpected, but it contributed to making 1963 a low point in my life. As is often the case, there was a silver lining to my political cloud. Shortly after the election my doctor informed me that I needed a hysterectomy. Had I been re-elected I probably would not have sought medical advice because I would have been too busy. Consequently, I would very likely not be alive today.

PART FOUR

Life after Politics

1963–1995

AT THE AGE OF FIFTY-EIGHT, most people begin to think of retirement, but not Ellen Fairclough. She helped make Hamilton Trust and Savings Corporation into a force to be reckoned with in Ontario financial circles and continued her active involvement in a wide range of boards, foundations, and voluntary organizations. With the death of Howard in 1986 and Gordon's subsequent illness, she was finally forced to cut back her commitments. Even then, she remained busy, making appearances on behalf of Progressive Conservative friends, writing her memoirs, and maintaining a hectic social life. In March 1995, she flew to Ottawa to be installed as a Companion of the Order of Canada by Governor General Roméo LeBlanc and participate in events organized to celebrate the occasion by the Ellen Fairclough Foundation, which was founded in 1986 to increase the role of women in the Progressive Conservative Party.

While Ellen was building a second business career, the women's movement emerged on the Canadian scene. The Liberal government under Lester Pearson (1963–8), pressed by women's groups, established a Royal Commission on the Status of Women in 1967. A whole new generation of women, schooled in the values of democracy and civil rights, was beginning to demand nothing less than total equality. Women formed pressure groups, marched, and even chained themselves to seats in the Gallery of the House of Commons to publicize their demands for everything from the legalization of abortion to equal pay for equal work. Although critics tried to trivialize the movement, they failed to deflect its main thrust. Women in North America had struggled under a double standard long enough, and even the most conservative women found something in the movement that spoke to their concerns.

Ellen Fairclough recoiled at some of the tactics of the 1960s feminists. As someone educated in the school of duty and compromise, she judged the new feminists too aggressive in their demands. Like many women of her generation, she approved the ends but not always the means and found herself saying, 'I am not a feminist but ...' She supported women such as Flora MacDonald and Kim Campbell, who were pushing back the frontiers for women in the Progressive Conservative Party, but she was not found in the ranks of the National Action Committee (NAC) or the Canadian Research Institute for the Advancement of Women (CRIAW).

In recognition of her pioneering achievements, Ellen received a growing number of accolades, particularly after the women's movement caught up to her in the 1970s. The list of honours, only some of which are discussed in this section, is impressive. While readers may find Ellen's chronicle of life after politics less revealing than her earlier chapters, it provides evidence of the wide range of her activities over the last thirty years and the esteem in which she is held in many circles.

Office staff of the Hamilton Trust and Savings Corporation; from left: Bob Anthony, Joanne Goudett, Dale Haverstock, Dawn Bresolin, Margaret Green, Janice McElroy, Donna Elmo, the author, and Michael Field

Named Advertising and Sales Person of the Year by Peter Frankland and Keith Garret of the Federation of Canadian Advertising and Sales Clubs, Kitchener, Ontario, 28 June 1969. (Photo by the *Kitchener-Waterloo Record*)

Dr Ellen Fairclough, McMaster University, 14 November 1975. (Photo by Joseph Bochsler)

Gordon at Fairclough Printing, April 1977. (Photo by *Hamilton Spectator*)

Inducted Officer of the Order of Canada by Governor General Ed Schreyer, Ottawa, April 1979. (Photo by John Evans)

With Robert Welch, unveiling the plaque for the Ellen Fairclough Building in Hamilton, 10 November 1982. (Photo by Dale Creasy)

With Gordon at my eightieth birthday party, 1 February 1985. (Photo by Sharon Godfrey)

With Flora MacDonald and Kim Campbell, 1993

With Grete Hale, first chair of the Ellen Fairclough Foundation, 1995.
(Photo by Denis Drever Photography)

With Monique Landry at Château Laurier Hotel, Ottawa, March 1995, celebrating my ninetieth birthday and installation as a Companion of the Order of Canada. (Photo by Denis Drever Photography)

8

Busy Days: Back to Business

It was becoming increasingly obvious that the Progressive Conservatives were not going to win the 1963 election. With a view to the future, Gordon Churchill suggested I should go to the Prime Minister and ask for a Senate appointment. When I approached John Diefenbaker I got a curt reply; despite being the first female cabinet minister, I was not to be one of the chosen few. Gordon Churchill was disgusted. Looking back, though, all I can say is, 'Thank God.' My subsequent career was much more exciting and gratifying than it would have been had the Prime Minister acceded to my request – another example of 'all things work together for good ...'

When it had begun to look as if I might not even win my own seat, I received a call from Allister Skinner. We had been friends since 1927, when he was a 'board boy' in W.H. Magill's brokerage office in Hamilton, where I was also employed. He urged me, if I should be defeated, not to make any decisions as to my future until I had consulted with him as spokesman for some of my friends. When the axe finally fell less than a year later, Al approached me again. He suggested I meet with Cameron MacGillivray to discuss my possible involvement in a new trust company to be based in Hamilton. After some thought on the matter and learning that most of the professional and business people behind the venture were friends or acquaintances, I accepted the invitation. The original members of the Board included Halliwell Soule, as President, W.E. Brunning, Murray G. Bulger, J. Ross Fischer, Norman G. James, George C. Knowles, George A. Miller, Charles A. Read, Philip Rosenblatt, William C. Schwenger, and Walter P. Thompson. My new life began in September 1963 when I became Corporate Secretary of the Hamilton Trust and Savings Corporation. Four years later I was appointed a Director, and eventually I served as Secretary-Treasurer and Vice-President.

My years with Hamilton Trust were the most enjoyable and personally satisfying of my business life. Under the presidency of Halliwell Soule, QC, and with the good advice of the Board of Directors, the company grew and flourished. We built several branches in Hamilton and then moved further afield to Brantford, Burlington, Grimsby, St Catharines, Stoney Creek, Tillsonburg, and Toronto. On 1 January 1978 we amalgamated with Canada Permanent. I sat on the Board of Canada Permanent until the calendar caught up with me in 1980; directors of financial institutions must retire at age seventy-five.

Other tasks came my way. In 1974 I was invited by Ontario Hydro to become a Commissioner of the Hamilton Hydro Electric System. The Commission is composed of three members – the Mayor, by virtue of his office; one person elected by the City Council (but not sitting on the current Council); and one appointed by Ontario Hydro, which I represented. It was a two-year term, and I was later reappointed several times and finally resigned in 1986, having served twelve years as a Commissioner, eight of them as Chairman. Members of the professional staff, under the leadership of General Managers Chesley K. Earle and James Hammond, taught me a great deal over the years.

Once out of political office, I was free to increase my involvement in voluntary organizations. A former member of my staff, June Alston, recruited me to the Board of the Miss Canada Foundation. June had moved from my office to Toronto, where she was employed in a promotional capacity by the Miss Canada Pageant. In the fall of 1963 she called on me at Hamilton Trust to ask if I would be a judge at the upcoming pageant. 'No way,' I replied. I would never judge a baby or a beauty contest, for it's a fine way to 'get your neck in a sling.' Refusing to take 'no' for an answer, she came back with the request that I serve on the Board of Directors of the Foundation itself, which was responsible for the scholarship monies won by the contestants. To this request I readily agreed – on the condition that the funds be deposited in Hamilton Trust and Savings. This condition was approved, and I chaired the Foundation for some ten years. The young women benefited both scholastically and artistically from the experience; their scholarship winnings were put to good use, and their training showed in the knowledge and poise they developed. CFTO-TV in Toronto produced the shows, and Ted Delaney, in particular, became a good friend.

Other opportunities beckoned. In 1977 Ralph Cooper, President of the Board of McMaster University Medical Centre Foundation, asked me to serve on his Board, which I agreed to do. The following year I accepted the post of Honorary Treasurer, which I retained after the amalgamation of the McMaster centre and Chedoke Hospital to operate under one administration as the Chedoke-McMaster Hospitals Foundation. In 1983 I was asked to take the newly created position of Executive Director of the Foundation on a 'quasi-honorary' basis. I worked out of an office with secretarial support and handled several 'housekeeping' jobs, as I called them, including financial management, advertising, and publicity.

During my tenure at the Foundation, Labatt's made life easier for a plodder like me. Its officer Suzanne Aziz gave financial support to the cause as well as advice on publicity. She put me in touch with Bern Wheeler, the communications expert, who helped us put out a quarterly report called *Health Pulse* as well as posters and brochures. In 1986, with a fund-raising campaign looming and my son's illness absorbing my emotional energy, I resigned the post of Executive Director; however, I remained on the Board and retained my title as Honorary Treasurer.

Several years earlier, William (Bill) McCulloch, manager of the Hamilton Chamber of Commerce, had stopped me on the street to say that I should become a member of that organization. I had not even considered it, I explained, because it was a 'man's organization,' but he said that was 'not necessarily so.' As a result I became the first woman to apply and be admitted to the Hamilton Chamber of Commerce. Earlier female members had been widows who had maintained their husbands' memberships. I became quite active, serving on the Hamilton Board, later the Ontario Board, and eventually the Canadian Chamber of Commerce, where I renewed my acquaintance with friends I had made through the Canadian Wholesale Grocers' Association.

I also continued my active participation in Zonta. In 1972 I was elected International Treasurer at a convention in Portland, Oregon. My Canadian friends Olga Cloke, Helen Cleveland, and Doris Tucker, from Toronto, and Marian Musselman, from Cambridge, were tireless in promoting my candidature and supported me with gusto when I was re-elected at the Boston convention two years later. Talented and dedicated women from many countries served on the International Board, and it was a pleasure to work with them.

The Zonta Club of Hamilton earlier had sponsored a special tribute to me as part of Canada's Centennial celebrations in 1967. Shortly after I was re-elected to Parliament in 1957, sculptor Elizabeth (Bradford) Holbrook asked if she could do my portrait. We had become acquainted through the United Empire Loyalist Association, to which her parents belonged. Continuing her studies and career while married to Dr John Holbrook and raising three children, she became an outstanding and well-known artist, winning international competitions and sculpting busts of such prominent people as Winston Churchill, John Diefenbaker, and Lester Pearson. Of course I was delighted that Betty wanted to sculp me. Since the House was in recess for the summer, we decided to use my office in the Centre Block for her studio; my departmental work could be done out of the Minister's office. With the assistance of the maintenance staff, the carpet was covered with a tarpaulin and a three-tier mirror was 'borrowed' from the sixth-floor lounge reserved for the use of parliamentary wives and their guests, who were not much in evidence during the summer. Betty came to Ottawa and shared my hotel room for a couple of weeks while she worked. Whenever I had a break, I ran over to my office and 'sat' for her. She then proceeded with the work until the next sitting. As can be imagined, the maintenance staff and others who knew she was there were intrigued by her work and called on her periodically to see how she was progressing.

When plans were being made for Canada's Centennial in 1967, the Zonta Club of Hamilton decided to procure the bust from Betty, who was also a member of Zonta, and sought permission from the Speaker of the House, Lucien Lamoureux, to have it installed in the Parliament Buildings. Permission was granted, and plans were made with the Zonta Club of Ottawa for a ceremony that took place in the Railway Committee Room on a bitterly cold day in February 1967. Despite the weather, the room was crowded with well-wishers, including twenty-six members of the Zonta Club of Hamilton, who braved the elements to attend, on a round trip of over six hundred miles. Mr Speaker Lamoureux presided, as a number of speakers, including John Diefenbaker, were introduced. Prime Minister Lester Pearson stole the show, when in the course of his remarks he turned to me and said, 'Well, I must say Ellen, it is a very cold day for you to unveil your bust.' The bust still sits in the Speaker's Gallery, near to the sculpture of Agnes Macphail.

Just recently, I learned of Betty's experience that day. She and her husband, Jack, were staying in the west end of Ottawa. Because of the bitter cold, their car would not start, and they could not secure a taxi because so many people had the same problem. Jack noticed a moving van, which had just deposited furniture in the neighbourhood, and he asked the driver if he was planning to pass near the Parliament Buildings. He agreed to take Betty as a passenger, so she arrived at the main entrance of the House of Commons in great style in a moving van. Such ingenuity!

Other forms of recognition also eventually came my way. For instance, in 1969 the Federation of Canadian Advertising and Sales Clubs began to recognize excellence in its field by naming some worthy individual the advertising and sales person of the year, and I was the first recipient of this award. In 1975, designated International Women's Year by the United Nations, I was among twenty-five women honoured by the province of Ontario for outstanding contributions to their community or country. Each of us received a scroll as well as an attractive trillium brooch fashioned from silver and amethyst mined in Ontario; after the brooches were produced, the die was destroyed. In the same year I received an honorary degree (Doctor of Laws) from McMaster University, and in 1978 I was named Chancellor of the Royal Hamilton Conservatory of Music, a happy appointment for someone who has always loved music and never had the chance to pursue it as much as I would have liked.

After Privy Councillor the highest distinction of all in Canada is the Order of Canada. On 22 December 1978 I received word that I had been named as an officer to the Order, and the following spring I attended the investiture, over which Governor General Ed Schreyer presided.

There seemed no end to the tributes. In 1982 William Davis, Premier of Ontario, asked me to agree to having the new Provincial Government building in Hamilton named for me. It was an astonishing request, and for once I was nearly speechless, but not for long. I readily agreed, and arrangements were made for 10 November. Robert Welch, Deputy Premier, officiated, with Deputy Minister of Government Services Allan Gordon acting as master of ceremonies. About seven hundred guests attended. Helen Bourke, then with the Department of Government Services, had made all the arrangements for the event and made sure that everything ran smoothly. Elizabeth Holbrook was contacted to produce a copy of the bronze bust in Ottawa. Clute Foster, an old friend, made available a pastel portrait of me by Nicholas Grandmaison, which was presented on his behalf by his son, Bruce Foster. Both works are now in the foyer at 119 King Street West, next to the Hamilton Convention Centre.

My eightieth birthday, on 28 January 1985, was celebrated quietly with my family at a private dinner in the Hamilton Club. On the following Friday, however, for reaching this important milestone I enjoyed a remarkably fine tribute at the Albany Club in Toronto. It was sponsored by 'The Committee for '94,' an all-party organization that spearheaded efforts to increase substantially the number of women in the House of Commons from the disappointing showing in the 1984 election. The affair was chaired by Libby Burnham and included Maude Barlow, Shirley Mann Gibson, Chaviva Hošek, Michele Landsberg, Christina McCall, Marcia McClung, Pauline McGibbon, Marilou McPhedran, Nadine Nowlan, Rosemary Speirs, Judy Steed, and Joyce Wieland. Speaking after dinner were Rosemary Brown, Iona Campagnolo, Christina McCall, Flora Mac-Donald, Alexa McDonough, and yours truly, the guest of honour. Over ninety people attended and we received messages from many friends. No men were invited. I received several threats, all in jest, that the affair would be picketed by males carrying signs, 'Unfair to Men.' Actually, Gordon was invited to the post-party reception.

Honours also came from my own city. In 1985 I was inducted into the Hamilton Gallery of Distinction. Under the auspices of the local Chamber of Commerce, each year six recipients are chosen, three of them deceased, so that outstanding citizens of former years also receive recognition. Since I was alive and kicking, I went to the ceremony. A portrait of each recipient is displayed at the Convention Centre. The year before, the Hamilton Women's Division of the State of Israel Bonds presented me with the Eleanor Roosevelt Humanities Award – a large bronze medallion – at a luncheon in the banquet hall of Adas Israel Synagogue. I received as well a magnificent golden-bound and illustrated volume of Holy Scriptures from the Beth Sholom Brotherhood of Toronto. Then, in February 1988, the Hamilton Status of Women Committee presented me with a citation in the form of a steel sculpture by Richard Kramer entitled *Nice Company*, which depicts a group of people in a very attractive design symbolizing friendship; a year later, I was a recipient of the Persons Award.

Further afield, at its annual dinner at the Royal York Hotel in Toronto on 5 November 1979, the Canadian Council of Christians and Jews presented me with a Human Relations Award in recognition of my contribution to community betterment. I had been a member of the Council's Board since 1950. And, in November 1993, at another ceremony in Toronto, the Churchill Society gave me an award recognizing excellence in the cause of parliamentary democracy. The guest speaker was Mary Soames, the only surviving child of Sir Winston Churchill. Although I had never before met Lady Soames, I had been presented to her father when he visited Canada in 1952.

Titles have also come my way. In 1985 the Knights Hospitaller of the Order of St John of Jerusalem (under the protection of the Crown of Yugoslavia) created me a Dame of Grace. And on 1 July 1992, in Ottawa, I was invested with the title 'The Right Honourable' in the presence of Her Majesty the Queen. On 22 December 1994, I was promoted to the rank of Companion of the Order of Canada, and the investiture took place at Rideau Hall in March 1995, soon after Roméo LeBlanc had assumed the position of Governor General.

In January 1995 I celebrated my ninetieth birthday, a milestone few people ever reach. Again, my friends were most generous. Joyce Mongeon hosted a pre-birthday dinner for me on 15 December 1994, inviting some twenty-five of our friends, both old and new, in the Hamilton area.

Perhaps best of all is to have one's achievements recognized by one's colleagues. On Monday, 20 February 1978, on the motion of Lincoln Alexander (Hamilton West), seconded by Erik Nielsen (Yukon), the House of Commons unanimously passed the following resolution: 'That the House extend its sincere congratulations to the Hon. Ellen Fairclough for the significant contribution she made to Canadian political life, for being, 20 years ago today, the only woman in Canadian political history to serve as Acting Prime Minister, and requests that the Speaker write a letter of congratulations to the Hon. Ellen Fairclough on this very significant anniversary.' Much had been made of the fact that in February 1958 John Diefenbaker left me in charge of the government as he went off on one of his junkets, and it was rather nice to have the occasion remembered.

Although I have never again run for political office, I have remained interested in the fortunes of the Progressive Conservative Party and was pleased when Robert Stanfield began the process of healing the rifts that had developed in the caucus following our defeat in 1963. I supported Donald Fleming for the party leadership in 1967 and nominated Lincoln Alexander as candidate for our party in my old riding in 1968. When he won the election, he again brought Hamilton West into national prominence, because he was the first black Canadian to sit in the House of Commons. Linc served briefly as Minister of Labour in Joe Clark's government and was appointed Lieutenant-Governor of Ontario in 1985.

Flora MacDonald ran for the party leadership in 1976 and I supported her. When she withdrew on the third ballot, I threw my support to Joe Clark; I was sorry to see him defeated in 1983. After that convention a number of Progressive Conservative women began to work to bring more women into the party. In 1986 the Ellen Fairclough Foundation was established to raise funds to support female candidates. I was recruited to be featured in a video to promote the cause (what a job that was!) and travelled to several parts of the country raising money for the Foundation.

The new generation of Progressive Conservative women has made a considerable impact. Both Flora MacDonald and Barbara McDougall served in the External Affairs portfolio, and Pat Carney was Minister of International Trade at the time of the Canada–United States free trade negotiations. When Kim Campbell ran for the leadership in 1993 I agreed to nominate her. Her success, though short-lived, brought women to new heights in political involvement and earned her a lasting place in our history books as the first female Prime Minister of Canada. Our party has come a long way since the 1920s, when I joined it. While I do not agree with all of its policies, I have remained a loyal member and hope that there are better days ahead.

As well as good fortune, we've had our share of tragedy over the years. Gordon was involved in a bad accident in 1980 when another car ploughed through a stop sign at Hess and Bold streets, crashed into the front of his car, then swung around and crashed into the back, causing over $4,000 worth of damage. Fortunately, it was a rented car and well covered by insurance. Although Gordon's head wound was easily patched up, he later developed a hernia which the doctors attributed to the seat belt.

In June 1986, he developed a hernia on the other side. Our physician, Dr Donald McLean, immediately sent him to a surgeon, who in turn recommended him to Dr William Goldberg for a heart examination. Of course, I tagged along. Afterward, the doctor instructed me to wheel Gordon in a chair right over to St Joseph's Hospital, where he was put under observation. The result, the implanting of a pacer, ruled out any operation in the near future. As is usual in such cases, Gordon was equipped with nitroglycerine pills and inhalants in case of an emergency.

Some months later, in February 1987, I was awakened in the night to sounds of distress and asked Gordon if he was all right. I grabbed the inhalant for him, but he could not manipulate it himself, so I shot some under his tongue. 'Give me five minutes,' he said, but at the end of that time he only felt worse, so I dialled emergency. I rushed to the clothes closet, grabbed a gown, and hurried down to the front door, by which time two ambulances were there. It could not possibly have been more than two minutes! I was amazed to find them there so promptly. The paramedics worked on him for about half an hour while they tried to find a bed for him in a hospital. After hearing 'no vacancy' two or three times, they finally located an opening at the Nora Henderson Hospital. Gordon said afterward that he did not think they would get him there in time. He was even unaware that I was riding with him in the ambulance. Nevertheless, in four days he was home again. It turned out that he had 'heart failure,' which necessitated draining water. I am convinced that the paramedics' prompt care saved him.

Unfortunately, their co-workers were unable to save Howard when he collapsed suddenly at his home in November 1986, just a week after his fifty-fifth birthday. He had been a heavy smoker for years and developed lung cancer. Despite an operation and subsequent treatment, the disease claimed its victim. A Requiem Eucharist celebrated at All Saints Anglican Church three days later was attended by several hundred friends and associates. The Province of Ontario was represented by Lieutenant-Governor Lincoln Alexander, and some thirty members of the Scottish Rite Singers led the music, with Lloyd Oakes at the organ. Special solos were provided by his close friend in the Scottish Rite, Oswald Lewis of Windsor. Howard's wife, Doreen, was a tower of strength through his illness, and it is sad that they had so few years together. It was a second marriage for both of them.

Gordon's heart condition was undoubtedly exacerbated by the grief he suffered because of Howard's death. From that time our lives have never been quite the same. There is a sadness deep in our hearts that comes from having your only child die before you.

9

Memories of a Saturday's Child

As I sat down to write my memoirs, it became obvious to me that the details of many so-called significant events – the fall of the Diefenbaker government, major policy innovations – had begun to fade from my memory. Other occasions, such as a luncheon with celebrities, a visit to a foreign country, a horrible gaff in public, had left much more vivid impressions on my mind. The fact that these highlights of public life were picked up by the media and preserved in photographs in my scrapbook no doubt accounts for this selective process. Of course, all the hoopla and preparations associated with public occasions – what to wear, who to invite, how to act – also helped to make them stand out.

One memorable affair occurred in 1956 when Dora Mavor Moore brought the revue *Spring Thaw* to Ottawa, where its members performed in the presence of the Governor General, Vincent Massey. I sat right behind Mr Massey in the theatre and enjoyed his amusement at the jibes directed at him. Because several of the cast were my son Howard's friends, I offered to host a luncheon for the cast in the private dining-room of the Parliamentary Restaurant. Many of those present, including Dave Broadfoot, Barbara Hamilton, and Robert Goulet, went on to exciting careers.

I like railway travel, especially on a private car. As a Minister of the Crown journeying on the nation's business, with several stops en route, I sometimes had a business car that doubled as an office and hotel for me and my staff. It was very comfortable and much more efficient than the inevitable packing and unpacking, taxis and tips, and the time-consuming routine entailed in moving from one hotel to another. Wherever we stopped we would be 'parked' in a railway yard and subsequently 'hooked up' on the end of the next train available, sometimes a freight. We inevitably caused considerable curiosity when we pulled into a station; onlookers would gather around and want to know who was on board.

Our favourite steward was Jimmy Sharland, who had been on royal trains and consequently displayed the crown on his cap. He knew all the tricks of his trade. As the train pulled into a station, he would pull the blinds and step outside, where he would stand with arms folded. On one such occasion, he repeatedly refused to comment to the onlookers, which only excited their curiosity. Just as the train was preparing to move, he said he would tell them who was behind the closed blinds if they wouldn't tell anybody else. Then, at the last possible moment, he informed them that the special train was for 'King Farouk.'

One of the most interesting aspects of public life is travel abroad. In the spring of 1958, Gordon Churchill, Sidney Smith, and I, accompanied by our spouses, made up the Canadian delegation to the ceremonies in Trinidad inaugurating the West Indies Federation. The heat was terrific and constant. Princess Margaret officiated and sat beautifully placid in the throne chair, which, we were told, had been specifically equipped with pipes at strategic positions to carry a flow of cold water. It must have been a great relief in the heat of a packed legislative chamber. Meanwhile, Gordon went through so many shirts in the few days we were there that he had to purchase a new supply locally.

We had a wonderful time exploring the island and learning the 'ropes.' Although Gordon managed to escape the street merchants who were hawking 'Bulova' watches that turned one's wrist green, Harold Shea, a correspondent with the *Halifax Chronicle-Herald*, was not so lucky. Back in the House of Commons, I would occasionally catch Harold's attention in the Press Gallery and look ostentatiously at my wrist, a performance that never failed to get a laugh from him.

The Canadian delegation hosted a reception at which our Trade Commissioner, R. Guy C. Smith, headed the reception line to introduce Gordon Churchill, who then introduced his wife; in turn she introduced me, then my husband, Sidney Smith and his wife, in that order, as precedence dictated. The line of visitors moved rather quickly as each person acknowledged the name and passed the guest along to the next person. Of course, it was sometimes difficult to hear the name of the guest distinctly. So it was that a 'distinguished gentleman' stopped in front of me; realizing that I had not caught his name from Mrs Churchill, he said, 'I'm the Prince Aly Khan,' whereupon I passed him on to Gordon, repeating the name but not registering for the moment who my guest had been. As he left the receiving line, it dawned on me, 'My goodness, that was the Aly Khan!' Later, he came over to talk to me, and we had a long discussion, mainly about Hamilton. He was interested in steel manufacturing and wanted to visit Canadian steel companies. He invited us to call on him in New York, which we did, and we were at the point of setting a date for his trip when his father's illness forced him to return home. While we were in his New York office, he talked at great length about his son, of whom he was exceedingly proud. I could not help but recall this occasion when his son, the Aga Khan, visited McMaster University and I had an opportunity to meet him.

Canada gave two ships to the West Indies Federation for inter-island use – the M.V. *Federal Palm* and the M.V. *Federal Maple*. On 26 August 1961 it was my job to christen and launch the *Federal Palm* at the Port Weller Dry Docks. I swung the traditional bottle of champagne on its long rope toward the ship's prow, but it was concave in shape and the bottle missed. It was hauled back, and I tried again and again until success was achieved on the fifth try. By this time the audience was in hysterics, and a tremendous cheer was raised when I finally succeeded. I don't think that I ever felt so foolish in my life. Fortunately, my failure to break the bottle did not bring the vessel bad luck, as superstition would have it. The *Federal Palm* is still plying the blue waters of the Caribbean, a tribute to the fine workmanship of Canadian boat builders, if not to my christening prowess.

During our visit to Trinidad, we met Grantley Adams, the Prime Minister of Barbados and the short-lived Federation. We later vacationed in Barbados several times, and each time had a visit – often a meal – with Sir Grantley, as he became, and his wife, Grace. We also met his son, Tom, who followed in his father's footsteps. Tom was elected to the Legislature and also became Prime Minister of Barbados, but died at a very young age. Sir Grantley died soon thereafter. During our last visit to Barbados in 1984, we talked to Lady Adams on the phone, but she was not well enough to visit us. We liked the Caribbean islands for vacations and enjoyed our visits to Antigua (several times), to Tobago (twice), and to Grenada (once).

At the suggestion of Lincoln Alexander, we made the acquaintance of Dr Luther Wynter and his wife, Arah, residents of Antigua. She was the daughter of Dr Barnes, who had been a podiatrist in Hamilton for many years.

Luther had a medical practice on Kenilworth Avenue. Because he was black, he was not well accepted in Hamilton. Indeed, he told us that he could not find a barber to cut his hair. When he received an offer from Antigua, he decided to accept it. He and Arah were married in Hamilton in the early 1920s and left for their new home. We visited them socially when we were on the island, and they came to our home when they were in Hamilton. He became a Senator, served as Deputy Governor, and was very popular in Antigua.

The last time we were in Antigua, Gordon got too much sun on the very first day – so much that his eyes swelled shut. We called Luther, who told us to get a taxi and come right over. Luther sent Gordon back with his eyes bandaged and instructions as to his care. Early the next morning, a Sunday, he telephoned to say he was coming over. He and Arah arrived about eight o'clock. Luther was walking with a cane, having fallen in the bathtub. We were touched by his thoughtfulness, particularly under the circumstances. It was because of Arah that we visited Grenada, where we were treated royally by their well-placed contacts on the island.

We also met interesting people at home. When Princess Margaret visited Canada in 1958, Gordon and I boarded her train at Niagara Falls. As the train approached Hamilton, we were summoned to the special coach on the end of the train to meet the Princess. Gordon's moment of glory came when the train made a sudden lurch, flinging Princess Margaret off balance. Gordon threw out his arms and caught her, which earned him a sweet smile and a 'thank you.'

In Hamilton, we accompanied the Princess as she presented colours to the regiment at Civic Stadium. On the way back to the train the royal car was greeted by crowds of well-wishers on both side of the street, waving, shouting, and throwing flowers into the open car. Princess Margaret continued waving in that half-armed way that both she and the Queen use on such occasions. A little later she turned to me and said in a light-hearted way, 'My arm is getting tired, you wave for a while.' I replied, to her amusement, 'I couldn't do that, Ma'am' – one addresses royalty this way – 'because these cheers are for you, but I'll be glad to hold up your arm like Moses.'

Some of the flowers actually landed in her lap. Although she did not like being hit by them, she picked up a few pink carnations and carried them to the train. She mentioned that her sister, during a visit to another country, was pelted with camellias to such an extent that she started throwing them back at the crowd.

Throughout the motorcade tour of Hamilton, the crowd shouted 'Hello Princess Margaret,' 'Hi Maggie,' and other greetings. She took it all with good grace, but she confessed to me, with a rueful smile, that she did not like being called 'Maggie.' It was, she said, what her family called her when they disapproved of her behaviour. I told her to let her family know that 'Maggie' was an endearing name in Canada and that henceforth she should not feel so badly about it. She also admitted that she disliked 'Marje' even more than 'Maggie' because she did not consider it a nickname for Margaret at all. When someone else yelled 'Atta girl,' she turned to me and said, 'Isn't that odd, I suppose that's an American expression.' Another word that intrigued her was 'doll.' Princess Margaret seemed to take everything in her stride. When I asked her to do so, she cheerfully waved at some of my friends leaning out of the windows at radio station CKOC at John and King streets.

The Princess was well briefed. As we turned out of the Stadium to go south on Melrose Avenue, the route was lined with men from the Argyll and Sutherland Highlanders, which she recognized. 'That's my sister's regiment,' she said. She asked about the First United Church when we passed it and made inquiries about the steel companies and the industrial area of the city. She said she would like to see the steel works, and I promised her that if she ever returned to Hamilton we would make sure she had a tour of both steel plants. Thirty years later, in 1988, her wish was granted; during a brief tour of Hamilton that year, Princess Margaret toured Dofasco and Stelco.

Also in 1958, in August, the International Convention of Fire Chiefs was held in Hamilton. One of the items on the program was the opening of a new Marine Warehouse at the foot of Wellington Street. George Hees, Minister of Transport, was on hand to open the facility, and I was invited, together with Gordon and Howard, to the luncheon that followed. During the meal, Hamilton's Fire Chief, Reg Swanborough, informed us that there were two new pieces of fire-fighting equipment outside and that he wanted George Hees and me each to drive one of them to the Royal Connaught Hotel, where the convention was being held. George was assigned to the aerial truck, and I was given a pumper!

When I climbed into the cab, I was joined by the truck salesman, who was obviously uncomfortable. The newsmen, of course, were having a field day. One of them remarked to Howard: 'Can your mother drive a truck?' to which he answered, 'Well, it has four wheels, hasn't it?' As I attempted to back up, I found that the gear shift was so stiff that I had to let go of the steering wheel and use both hands to move it. I had visions of what would happen if this procedure continued, so I said to the salesman, 'Look, I'll clutch and you shift gears.' He readily agreed and relaxed enough to ask me if I had ever driven a Cab-over engine. When I answered in the negative, he said: 'Oh well, you'll have to cut it sharp when you turn or you'll land on the lawn across the street.' I managed to do as I was told, and after that we got along just fine.

Accompanied by an escort of several motorcycle policemen, with me in the lead, we proceeded along the two-mile drive to the Connaught. Standing on the sides of my truck were Quinto Martini, MP for Hamilton East, and Robert (Bob) McDonald, MP for Hamilton Mountain. At one point I came so close to a telephone pole that Bob McDonald feared he would be 'brushed off.' Fortunately, everything went without a hitch. I would never have heard the end of the 'lady driver' jokes if I had been unable to carry out this public duty. Later George asked me how I managed to get so far ahead of him. He confessed that every time he changed gears he had to slow down and take both hands off the steering wheel to accomplish the task. I told him that I had employed a technique from my courting days when, with his arm around my shoulders, Gordon operated the clutch and I would shift gears! At the reception, HM the Queen's Fire Chief, visiting from England, complimented me on 'an excellent performance,' and assured me that if I came to London I would have a job.

One extraordinary incident in my political life must be recounted for the record. Around eleven o'clock one evening I returned to my room in the Chateau Laurier and noticed a couple of RCMP officers standing in the hallway. I thought nothing about it because the Mounties were usually around when there was an important person in a nearby suite. However, the next morning, as I was finishing my breakfast (which I always had in my room to save time), there came a knock on my door. On my answering it, a large black man marched into the room and asked, 'Is the Prime Minister here?' On seeing no evidence of his quarry, he proceeded to look around, even in the closets and bathroom. Then, without a word, he turned on his heel and strode out of the room. To say I was surprised and perplexed would be a massive understatement.

When I arrived at a cabinet meeting a short time later, I asked if anyone knew who was in town. 'Yes, Patrice Lumumba, the Prime Minister of the Congo,' was the answer, so I told my colleagues what had happened. Diefenbaker was not in the room but someone must have told him later. He loved a good story and would not let me forget that Lumumba's aide came to my room to look for his boss. Lumumba stayed for about a week and was the subject of considerable discussion because his retinue, his demands, his costly habits (Canada had to pay the bills), and his flamboyant behaviour were all larger than life. Whenever Lumumba's name came up, Dief would nod in my direction and say, 'Your friend!,' which never failed to get a laugh from my colleagues.

Someone, probably Diefenbaker himself, also told news columnist Charles Lynch. He and Dief would have had a good time embroidering the incident to the point where it was truly hilarious. I had forgotten all about it until Charlie's book *You Can't Print THAT!* was published in 1983. He sent me an autographed copy, and, true enough, he presented the tale in a much exaggerated form. Among my friends, I was forced to tell the right story many times to restore my good reputation. I wrote to Charlie, telling him that his version was completely false and that if I ever wrote a book I would refute it.

Charlie addressed the Canadian Club in Hamilton while I was an officer of that body. We inevitably bumped into each other at a reception prior to the luncheon. He announced that he intended to retell the story; did I have any objection? I replied, 'No,' but added, 'You know perfectly well, Charlie, that you manufactured that story out of whole cloth and there is not a word of truth in it.' He acknowledged that was so but said that it was a great tale anyway and that he had 'earned many a good meal' on recounting this fictitious incident.

The story that he told involved my (supposed) attendance at a reception that Howard Green, Secretary of State for External Affairs, had given, to which in fact I was not invited. It was customary for the staff to canvass Ministers, on the visit of a foreign dignitary, or any other important function, to find out who was available to represent the government. It was impossible for Ministers to be present at all such functions because of other duties, so there would be four or five in attendance for any given state occasion. Since I had not 'booked' the Lumumba visit, I was not one of those who attended the reception. Indeed, I did not even know that he was in town.

I would not have belaboured this point except for the fact that a friend called me to say that Charlie's version of the story was reprinted in the *Oxford Book of Canadian Political Anecdotes* (1988). Once in print, it seems, it never dies. I do not expect that this rather prosaic version of the Lumumba visit will kill Charlie's story, which is much more amusing than mine – at least for some people – but this is, in any event, 'for the record.'

Also 'for the record,' I should describe the sorts of incidents often put forward to show the degree of discrimination faced by a woman in the 'men's world' of politics. It is true that I often had to go long distances in the Parliament Buildings to find a women's washroom. There are accounts of valiant colleagues standing guard outside the men's washroom just outside the cabinet room door, while I used the 'facilities.' Although there may have been times when their chivalry was called upon, it was usually the steward outside our meeting room who performed such duties.

Early in my career as a cabinet minister, the top brass of Toronto-Dominion Bank, as was their custom, hosted a luncheon for the cabinet at the Rideau Club in Ottawa. Since there had never been a woman in the cabinet, the fact that the Rideau Club was closed to women had posed no problems for earlier celebrations. I did not, as has sometimes been claimed, even try to get into the luncheon. I just wrote a little note thanking them for the invitation but saying that, for obvious reasons, I would be unable to attend. When our hosts realized the implications of their choice of venue, they sent enough flowers to my room in the Château Laurier to dignify a state funeral.

Only once did the fact that I was a woman cause me to be excluded from cabinet deliberations. The death penalty was still occasionally imposed, and appeals were made directly to cabinet. As it turned out, the last such case was that of Stephen Truscott, who had been convicted of a murderous sexual assault. When the case came before cabinet, the documents included a number of graphic photographs of the deceased. Diefenbaker turned to me and said, 'Now Ellen, this is a matter we have to discuss and I suggest you leave.' I did so willingly – not in tears, as some have claimed – because I was requested to do so by the Prime Minister of Canada. However, I could see no reason, other than the discomfort of the men, as to why I should be excluded. The incident was more amusing than annoying and revealed a rather old-fashioned side to Diefenbaker's personality.

In a number of accounts of events during the Diefenbaker years, including this one, it is recorded that Ellen Fairclough wept. I am rarely reduced to tears, especially in public, so such reports are purely wishful thinking on the part of men who want to embellish their story. I certainly did not leave the cabinet meeting in tears over the Truscott matter.

On a general level, I did not let discriminatory behaviour get under my skin. I had been working for many years with business associations where I was the only woman and had learned to adjust to such situations long before I entered politics. My business colleagues treated me as just 'one of the boys,' and I did not notice much difference in the political world. Of course, I may have been excluded from some of the behind-the-scenes activities in the party, but there were a lot of men outside the inner circle, too. My political strength was in administrative organization, not political manoeuvring, and most of my colleagues understood that.

An invitation to address the Soroptimist Club of Timmins in September 1960 resulted in an unusual adventure. During our visit, we were royally entertained both by the mayor and council at luncheon and by the managers of the fourteen mines in the Timmins-Porcupine area. There were the usual interviews by press, radio, and television, but the high point of the trip was an extended tour of the Hollinger Mine, both above and below ground. I met the workers, many of whom were new Canadians, as they came off shift, and then – suitably protected by hard hat and overalls – descended to the working level, where I was instructed on the operation of a jackleg rock drill. I had to be outfitted in men's clothing several sizes too big, especially the boots. Gordon and Kingsley Brown, who accompanied me on the trip, got a great kick out of my new 'look.' Yours truly, complete with overalls and hard hat, was featured on the cover of the October 1960 issue of the *Hollinger Miner*, a magazine for the firm's employees. Before we left, our hosts suggested that I 'pour' a gold bar. I did so with the assistance of Edward Hunt, the furnace operator. I was the butt of the usual joke when they told me that I could have a gold bar – just pick it up. I forget how much they weighed, but certainly far more than I could lift.

This was a memorable visit for another reason as well, for I met Mary

Copps, the mother of Hamilton mayor Victor Copps and grandmother of Sheila Copps, now a Member of Parliament and Deputy Prime Minister in Jean Chrétien's Liberal government. Mary raised six sons single-handedly after the death of her husband, working as a school teacher and later as a court reporter. Her triumph in the face of adversity no doubt inspired other women in her family.

Politicians are expected to be larger than life and to be able to sustain the most gruelling schedules without wilting. The following is an example of how one's life unfolds as a Minister of the Crown. Shortly after Georges Vanier had taken office as Governor General in 1959, I was invited to dinner at Rideau Hall. The party broke up about 11:15 p.m. When I arrived back at the hotel, I ran into Wally Nesbitt in the lobby. He accepted my invitation for a nightcap but had to make a stopover at the Lord Elgin Hotel first. By the time he got back and we had our confab over drinks, I finally got to bed at 1:30 a.m. The next day I had to be at Malton Airport in Toronto for the arrival of the first group of TB refugees and their families. I arose at the ungodly hour of 6:00 a.m. (I hate getting up early) and was ready for Monte Monteith when he picked me up at 7:30 to go to the airport. We had a Department of Transport Viscount, so we arrived at Malton at 9:15, to find that the Canadian Pacific Airlines plane was not expected until 10:30. However, press, radio, and television interviews took up the time. At 10:30 we all went out to the plane to greet the newcomers as they came down the ramp. The official party included me as Minister of Citizenship and Immigration, Monte as Minister of Health and Welfare, and Dr Dymond as provincial Minister of Health. There were also deputy ministers and other officials, to the number of about ten persons, and countless photographers – still, TV, and movie. The photographing went on for about three-quarters of an hour. I felt sorry for these poor people who had just flown the Atlantic and were undoubtedly tired. To go through the ordeal of questions and prodding must have been the last straw. You could see their exhaustion. Nevertheless, they were wonderful about it, probably because they were all somewhat bewildered by the attention and few, if any, could speak more than a few dozen words of English.

We managed to get away about noon, flying right back to Ottawa. I was in my office by two o'clock. That evening I hosted a dinner party at the Moodies', serving two snow geese that Thomas Maher, Chairman of the

Board of the National Gallery, had kindly sent me. Daisy and Jim were their usual, hospitable and charming selves, and the food was delicious. It was prepared by Noel Villeneuve and served by Flo Russel, both of whom worked at the Parliamentary Restaurant. All the rest of us had to do was enjoy ourselves. My guests were Arthur White (*Time* magazine), Jim Nelson (PM's office), the Sam Rosses (radio), and the Sam Hugheses (Civil Service Commission). They went home around 11:30 p.m. at which time the Moodies informed me that they were invited to visit Ed and Mary Houston and I was asked to come too. Although we decided that we would not stay very long, by the time we got there and back it was 2:00 a.m. As I said at the time, 'Typical.'

My cabinet colleagues were a fractious lot, but we also shared a sense of humour, which sustained us through the most difficult times. The Prime Minister frequently indulged in witty asides, which were sometimes delightful but often pretty caustic. After one journalist, known as Moon, criticized us for appointing Murdo McPherson to the chairmanship of the Royal Commission on Freight Rates, because he was known to be pro-provinces and anti-railways, Dief's eyebrows rose. Someone said that the article was so vicious that Moon could be sued for libel. With a perfectly dead-pan expression, the PM said quietly, 'That would be the height of Luna(r)cy.'

In February 1960 Charlotte Whitton was taken to hospital for an emergency operation. As is often the case in these matters, there was great secrecy with regard to details. I suspected that it was merely appendicitis, but Charlotte had her press relations people working overtime, and the general impression was that it was more serious than that. Many people, especially men, found Charlotte rather intimidating. While her health was the subject of much speculation, Doug and Frances Harkness gave a reception to which I was invited. Seeing Grattan O'Leary, I asked him if he knew the nature of Charlotte's illness. He said, 'No, but to my great consternation, I find it's not serious.' I said, 'Well, I thought you would know if anyone did, and it all seems very mysterious.' He replied, 'No, I don't know, but when I first heard it, I was sure it must be prostate.'

(Subsequently, Charlotte's sister Ryan told me that it was a twisted bowel, which was straightened out without too much difficulty. My original suspicion had a basis in fact, because at the same time they removed her appendix also.)

Don Fleming was considered a dry stick by many of our more exuberant cabinet colleagues, but he also had a sharp wit. One day George Nowlan was late for cabinet, a misdemeanour that always earned a black look from Dief. Nowlan was not easily intimidated. As he strolled to his seat, he remarked that Charlie Van Horne, the maverick Progressive Conservative member for Restigouche-Madawaska, had decided to sit as an Independent. There was some murmuring, and then someone said in mock alarm, 'What do you think we should do?' The answer came from Don Fleming, who, in his drollest manner, replied, 'I suggest that we all rise and sing the Doxology.'

The long cabinet meetings became tiresome, and sometimes someone would fall asleep. On the odd occasion, nearly everyone seemed afflicted, probably due to a combination of long hours, monotonous and lengthy discussions, and poor ventilation. We had the bright idea one day that we would all chip in to buy a coffee thermos and some cups so that we could slip out to the ante room, now and then, for a cup of coffee. One time someone asked Dave Walker, Minister of Public Works, if he wasn't coming out for coffee. He replied, 'No, I don't want any coffee. It might keep me awake!' Imagine buying one's own coffee equipment! Today's cabinet would think we were out of our minds.

Dief kept a pretty tight rein on us. The following is the text of a news broadcast over radio station CFRA in Ottawa, 3 July 1961:

PRIME MINISTER HAS TURNED TRUANT OFFICER
CFRA News has learned that about fifty members of Parliament left Ottawa Friday night for their homes in the Prairie Provinces. Mr Diefenbaker became angry with his MPs for playing hookey, and sent an urgent message to Agriculture Minister Hamilton and Defence Minister Harkness, who were in Winnipeg, to intercept the men and send them back. The two cabinet ministers met the MPs in Winnipeg and relayed the message. It is not known what followed the instructions, but Mr Diefenbaker was not there to meet them. The PM is in Toronto to speak to the annual convention of Kiwanis International.

Naturally we had had more time for fun when we sat in Opposition. There was always something amusing happening and an occasion – somebody's birthday, a by-election win, anything – was an excuse for a party. Angus MacLean, Gordon Churchill, and I composed rhymes and set them to music for the benefit of our colleagues. I still have a little book of limericks that the three of us composed about members of the Liberal caucus. Angus MacLean and Henri Courtemanche had beautiful voices that did real justice to our doggerel. Such events were delightful and contributed to the spirit of camaraderie that carried us over a good many rough spots. Once in office, we had little time for celebrations and our caucus was too large for the kind of intimacy that we shared in Opposition.

When I moved to the Department of Citizenship and Immigration, I was told that we held in storage a table that was reputed to have been used by Sir John A. Macdonald when he was Superintendent General of Indian Affairs. (Incidentally, I was the thirty-second person to hold that position.) I asked to see it and found it to be in good, solid condition but scruffy from years of use and storage. It seemed foolish to leave it to gather more dust, so I decided to have it refinished. On the border we placed a brass plate indicating that the table had belonged to Sir John A. and the dates of his tenure as Superintendent General. I then made an appointment with the Prime Minister and presented him with the historic table. Diefenbaker was delighted with it. He called in reporters and cameramen, who took pictures and listened to his anecdotes about Sir John, some of which they had undoubtedly heard many times before. I wonder where the table is now?

Throughout my career in business and politics I have had several 'doubles' and am frequently called by someone else's name – I presume they are also confused with me. The one I resemble most closely is Olga Cloke, an acquaintance of mine through Zonta. So far as we know there is absolutely no relationship, but the likeness has led to many amusing situations. Another double really did cause me some trouble. This woman lived in the downtown area of my federal constituency of Hamilton West and was a frequenter of several bars. When someone would ask her, 'Aren't you Ellen Fairclough?' she would respond, 'Sure, have a drink!' Apparently she could well afford to pay the bill, but we had to hunt her down and ask her to desist. It had never occurred to her that, in the midst of a campaign, this behaviour might cause me some embarrassment.

As far as identifying others goes, public life has its advantages, one being the 'whisper in the ear.' After my defeat in 1963, I was invited to speak at a luncheon in the Town Hall in New York. Our Consul-General was Ray

Lawson, who had been the Lieutenant-Governor of Ontario. He was out of town, so Mrs Lawson represented him. When we assembled at the head table, I remarked to her that it felt odd to be walking ahead of her. As wife of the Lieutenant-Governor, she had always taken precedence over me. We chuckled over our reversed status and continued to reminisce about highlights in our political careers. At one point I asked her what she missed, if anything, about her former post. She replied, 'having someone whisper names into my ear.' I can well understand her response, because it is embarrassing to be unable to recall a name one should know and very nice to have assistants to keep one well informed.

Earl Rowe used to tell a delightful story about a member of the Ontario Legislature, Herb Lennox, who had a large garden party on his farm each summer. Howard Ferguson was the Premier and guest of honour. While the two were conversing on the lawn, Mr Lennox observed a woman purposefully walking toward them, and, try as he would, he could not remember her name. As she came near, expecting to be introduced, Mr Lennox said, 'Oh, what a coincidence, Mr Premier, here is the lady I was just telling you about.' Then, he turned on his heel and walked away, leaving the Premier to find out her name for himself.

In the course of my life I have given or listened to thousands of speeches. There were debates, after-dinner musings, public speaking contests, electioneering, sermons, historical discourses, eulogies, etc., etc., etc. Some I have enjoyed, some have amused me, and others I have endured. Most speakers have 'borrowed' from other speakers and writers, with or without acknowledgment. I once read an article that described a speech given by a gentleman somewhere in California. I was greatly interested to find that he had faithfully produced as his own the whole text of an address I had made some months previously in Chicago. I hasten to add that it had been entirely original with me. However, I have done my share of quoting of others but have tried to give credit where credit is due.

Once I did not do so! When asked by the United Empire Loyalist Association to address an important meeting, I remembered a speech given by James M. Sinclair, a friend from my wholesale days. He was a very witty individual, and a paragraph of his remarks fitted right in with the theme of my address, so I 'appropriated' it. After the event, the sponsors asked permission to publish my remarks for general distribution. I was flattered, but, with belated recognition of my indebtedness, I wrote to Jim and told him what I had done, facetiously asking if he intended to sue me for plagiarism.

In his reply he recounted the story of a hillbilly who wanted to get married, but every time he told his father the name of his intended bride the father would say, 'You can't marry her, she's your half-sister.' After about three tries, the young man went to his mother, who was deeply involved with the family washing in the back yard. He told her his story, whereupon she straightened up, sloshed the suds from her arms, and said, 'Honey-chile, you go ahead and marry whoever you like 'cause that there hillbilly ain't your pappy.' Jim's response to my dilemma was then, 'Honey-chile, you go ahead and use whatever you like 'cause it ain't my brain-chile.' I think it's called literary licence – plagiarism, that is!

It would be difficult to plagiarize a life like mine, one full of achievement as well as failure. Although I never started out to be the 'first' anything, it turned out that I was the first woman in many areas of public life. There were not many others to follow, so I just followed my own instincts. These served me pretty well over the years, as did my willingness 'to work hard for a living.' And when all is said and done, it has been a pretty satisfying life.

Index